A celebration of the splendor and struggles of marriage! The stories of real couples will move you, the practical suggestions will educate you, the quotations sprinkled throughout will get you thinking, and the authors' own marital journey will inspire you.

William Doherty, Ph.D., author of *Take Back Your Marriage*

Great warmth, wisdom, and practical application! Weaving the wisdom of the past with heart-warming contemporary stories, this book stands head and shoulders above the rest. Extremely pragmatic, with valuable tools for improving marriages, this book is a great one. I recommend it highly.

Frank Minirth, M.D., Diplomate American Board of Psychiatry and Neurology

Every marriage, no matter how good, bumps into difficulties. And this book can help you absorb those bumps with more grace and agility than you thought possible.

Dr. Les Parrott and **Dr. Leslie Parrott**, authors of *When Bad Things Happen to Good Marriages*

Great storytellers, Maureen and Lanny Law give us stories of love and loss, most poignantly their own, from which we can learn much about how to keep a relationship strong in spite of everyday stresses and unexpected tragedies. Bravo!

Pauline Boss, Ph.D., author of *Ambiguous Loss: Learning to Live With Unresolved Grief*

There is no better teaching tool than an aptly told story. The carefully selected, well-crafted and tender stories in this book will resonate, bring hope, and teach about paths to a healthy, committed marriage.

Sara Wright, Ph.D., American Association for Marriage and Family Therapy Board Member

Honest and reflective, this book has something to say to everyone. It offers great insight on how couples can cope with anything that life throws at them. A successful American Irish love story!

Adrian Flannelly, Host, Irish Radio Network, USA

This wonderful book should be read by couples whose relationships are satisfying as well as by those who are facing difficulties. Marital therapists and counselors should recommend this book to all their clients . . . a gem!

Dr. Alan Carr, Director of Clinical Psychology Training, University College, Dublin

Inspiring, challenging, and informative! Couples at any stage can benefit from the antidotes and exercises it offers.

Donna and **Glen Hambleton**, Association of Couples for Marriage Enrichment Board Members

A living testament of the loving and learning of a married couple who are also therapists. They discovered twelve core relationship principles that come alive with revealing personal stories and quotes. A treat to read for all couples.

David H. Olson, Ph.D., Professor Emeritus, University of Minnesota, author of *Empowering Couples: Building on Your Strengths*

Marriage is a risky undertaking. This book gives practical, helpful advice on how to resist being overwhelmed. It affirms people's ability to make a difference in their marital circumstances by sharing stories of couples who honor each other's differences, understand and resolve their conflicts, and learn how to offer—and receive—forgiveness.

Dr. Andrew Pierce, Irish School of Ecumenics, Trinity College, Dublin

Why do we need yet another book on marriage? Because Maureen and Lanny Law have given us one with both sound theory and powerful real life narratives. They enrich our understanding of married life and give us incentives to change behaviors.

George Brushaber, Ph.D., President, Bethel College and Seminary, St. Paul, MN

So often couples seek specific steps and interventions to resolve their conflicts and impasses. The authors have set forth a model that is understandable, useful, and effective. A remarkable job with a complex topic!

Charme Davidson, Ph.D., ABPP, President of the Minnesota Association for Marriage and Family Therapy

God Knows
Marriage
Isn't Always
Easy

12 ways to add zest

Maureen Rogers Law and Lanny Law

SORIN BOOKS Notre Dame, IN

Other Titles in the *God Knows* Series

God Knows You're Stressed:
Simple Ways to Restore Your Balance

God Knows You'd Like a New Body:
12 Ways to Befriend the One You've Got

God Knows You're Grieving:
Things to Do to Help You Through

God Knows We Get Angry:
Healthy Ways to Deal With It

As publisher of the *GOD KNOWS* series, SORIN BOOKS is dedicated to providing resources to assist readers to enhance their quality of life. We welcome your comments and suggestions, which may be conveyed to:

SORIN BOOKS
P.O. Box 1006
Notre Dame, IN 46556-1006
Fax: 1-800-282-5681
e-mail: sorinbk@nd.edu

www.sorinbooks.com

International Standard Book Number: 1-893732-29-0

Cover and text design by Katherine Robinson Coleman

Cover photo by Rubberball

Printed and bound in the United States of America.

Library of Congress Cataloging-in-Publication Data

Law, Lanny.
God knows marriage isn't always easy : 12 ways to add zest / Lanny Law and Maureen Rogers Law.
      p. cm.
ISBN 1-893732-29-0 (pbk.)
1. Marriage. 2. Marriage--Religious aspects--Christianity. I. Law, Maureen Rogers. II. Title.
HQ734 .L3367 2002
646.7'8--dc21

2001005239
CIP

CONTENTS

Introduction

Having a healthy marriage is one of life's greatest blessings.

In a thriving marriage, wife and husband are energized and can withstand just about any circumstances they face. As they move through life, each is blessed with a special companion, a best friend, a lover, a confidant—someone who calls forth from them all that is best in who they are.

However, other couples feel imprisoned in unhappy marriages. Despair, anger, fear, anxiety, and hatred fester. When a couple is living an unhappy marriage their growth is stifled, both collectively and individually. Their energies are drained away in bitter recriminations, and they have difficulty facing the challenges of life. Instead of the marriage making life easier and more rewarding, the relationship is destructive and only makes life more difficult.

For most of us, our marriages go along smoothly enough between these two extremes. We deal with the challenges of marriage the best ways we know how, realizing that we could do better and sure that we could do much worse. Getting married, staying married, and becoming happily married is a journey that may have detours, roadblocks, and breakdowns, so most of us stay aware that we can learn other ways to enrich our relationship.

God Knows Marriage Isn't Always Easy: 12 Ways to Add Zest is a helpful guide of twelve ways for couples to work out some of the simple and not-so-simple roadblocks that crop up in any marriage. In our work as psychotherapists, we have helped others—not to mention ourselves—use these twelve ways to improve their relationships. Sometimes when people get discouraged about the state of their marriage a friendly dose of stories, insightful words, and well-timed guidelines can rekindle the sparks of their relationship. We hope that the ideas and stories in this book can encourage you to improve your own marriage.

Twelve Ways to Improve Your Relationship

The twelve ways we suggest for improving your relationship (adding zest!) are all necessary elements to having a better marriage. In this book, we introduce these twelve ways by sharing real stories of how they have impacted our own marriage and the marriages of people we have known or counseled. Briefly, the twelve ways are:

- *Meet and Do Things Together* Lanny grew up in Minneapolis; Maureen in Dublin, Ireland. Our relationship, as long distance as it may appear, was formed by doing things together. It has grown through the years by sharing in activities together.

- *Accept the Similarities and Differences in Each Other* As we grew closer, we became aware of both our similarities and our differences in several areas including culture, personality, beliefs, family of origin, and hobbies. By accepting each other's differences we discovered they enriched our relationship.

- *Strive to Understand Each Other* Understanding each other involves taking the necessary time to clarify and discover each other's messages, both spoken and unspoken.

- *Choose to Feel Each Other's Emotions* Having feelings for the other, being open to the feelings of the other, and caring about what each is feeling is crucial to our growing together.

- *Mindfully Nurture Your Love* Expressing our good will toward one another helps to deepen the relationship.

- *Make Your Relationship Priority Number One* Placing our marital partnership ahead of our parents, our friends, and our work relationships brings growth in our relationship.

- *Delight One Another With Touch* Holding, embracing, kissing, and making love communicate our love for one another in both body and spirit.

- *Consciously Balance Togetherness and Uniqueness* When each of us cares about our own interests while still paying to attention to the other's desires, we develop a sense of fairness, which contributes to a healthy relationship.

- *Help One Another* In marriage, we strive to be "helpmates" to one another, that is, looking for ways we can lighten the other's load.

- *Resolve Conflicts Before They Get Worse* When there is disagreement, feelings of irritation, frustration, and anger arise. Resolving conflicts quickly and honestly is crucial for a marriage to thrive.

- *Readily Forgive and Reconcile If Possible* Even when we do hurt each other, we have the opportunity to forgive one another, and when the one who is hurt is willing and able, to reconcile as well.

- *Share Each Other's Joys and Sorrows* Sharing the low ebbs of our partner's life can actually deepen the bonds of marriage when we let it.

In summary, we have a better marriage when we practice the following elements in our relationship: meeting, accepting, understanding, feeling, loving, prioritizing, touching, balancing, helping, resolving, forgiving, and sharing. The chapters ahead feature stories and several suggestions for using each of these valuable ways to improve your relationship.

Words of Thanks

In writing this book, we have many to thank. First of all we want to thank our parents for the positive role models they have been for us. Now deceased, John and Maureen Rogers (Dublin, Ireland) were loving partners for over fifty-five years of marriage. Arlene and Loren Law (Minneapolis, Minnesota) have been married for over sixty years, and remain loving companions.

We also thank our children—Erin, Christine, Kevin, and Kathleen—for patiently putting up with us as we devoted many evening and weekend hours to writing this book in the last year. We also remember our son Sean who died in 1987.

We thank the many couples we have known who have demonstrated the traits of a positive marriage relationship. We want to thank the professors, writers, and colleagues who have clarified ideas of healthy marriages for us. We were fortunate to spend some time at a leaders' retreat on marriage enrichment with David and Vera Mace. We were able to observe firsthand in their lives the core concepts of a healthy, happy marriage. Through the years their writings have had a major impact on our own view of marriage.

We thank the many individuals and couples for whom we have provided psychotherapy. The ideas we have about marriage have been used, tested, and refined as we helped our patients improve their relationships. In the stories we have shared in this book, we have changed identifying details to protect their confidentiality and in some cases have combined two or more stories into one.

We want to thank our editor, Carl Koch, for his guidance, and to Sorin Books for giving us the opportunity to share our beliefs about marriage. These twelve principles are found in the Bible and many of them can be helpful to any human relationship as well as marriage. For this reason, we also thank God.

Ideally, we hope that this book will be read by both wives and husbands. In doing so, we hope that you will be inspired and encouraged so that you will talk about what is being presented. Try not to hurry through the book. Take your time and let the ideas help you on your journey together.

WAY 1 :

Meet and Do Things Together

JUST HAVING FUN TOGETHER NOT
ONLY LIGHTENS STRESS, BUT ALSO
BUILDS A BRIDGE BETWEEN YOU LIKE
NOTHING ELSE. BE FUNNY; GIVE
YOURSELVES A LOT TO LAUGH
ABOUT. AND DO IT AS A COUPLE.

Tim Clinton

Doing things together seems such an obvious way to maintain a successful relationship, nevertheless it is not uncommon for many couples to cease all common activities after many years of marriage. Every day couples have a chance to vitalize their relationship by doing things together. When we do, we learn about each other and develop a friendship. We learn what the other likes and dislikes.

The type of activity isn't as important as just doing things together: walking in the park, sharing a meal, cuddling on the couch, or painting the living room together. Getting together to visit friends or going out on a date to a game, play, museum, or numerous other types of activities deepens our relationship.

Ted and Ann were happy when they were dating each other. They shared a lot of activities together, but they also had some interests outside of their relationship. While still single and living apart, they would see each other almost every day, but still had some independence. Since they married, they have experienced tension.

Now in their second year of marriage, they thought they would be blissfully happy, but ongoing tensions and strife have prevailed. They came in for counseling after Ann told Ted that she wanted a separation. They were feeling disconnected and spent less and less time together. When they *were* together they bickered. Sadly, they had discovered that it wasn't so much fun to be together, so they found excuses to be apart. They would often go to bed at different times and sometimes eat separately.

As they looked at their relationship, Ann and Ted started to realize that avoiding each other only compounded their problems. So I encouraged them to spend some time together initially just doing some common activities without trying to fix all of their problems. After that, I told them they could begin addressing their issues.

So, they ate together again, watched television, and did other ordinary things that couples usually do. Almost immediately Ted and Ann felt more hopeful as they addressed their issues. The primary issue, it turned out, was their different understandings of independence. Early on, Ann was so much in love with Ted that months passed before she realized that she missed her female friends and her independence. After the sixth month of marriage, she told Ted of her desire to see some of her friends.

Since Ted did not feel the need to connect to his old buddies, he did not understand her desire to spend some time apart from him. During our sessions, Ann expressed that she had even gone back to college part-time and began working more hours just to have an excuse to get some time away from Ted. He seemed okay with the time she was spending away from him if it was for school or work. But he didn't understand her desire to be with her friends.

For Ann, the issue came to a head when she told him, "Ted, I love you and I love being with you. I just want some time to do some things without you." Her declaration lowered Ted's anxiety, and he was able to back up and accept the space she desired. Now, when Ann is able to spend some time with her friends, she comes home with more enthusiasm for Ted. No longer does she find herself trying to avoid him.

Ann began to let Ted be himself, too. He liked spending time enjoying his hobbies. But since he had become used to solitude, Ann has had to initiate activities as a couple. Now they are learning how to enjoy one another again.

How much time and what activity a couple does together depends on the two unique individuals in the relationship. The important element remains, however, that they actually need to do things together.

Our relationship was formed, maintained, and deepened by sharing activities together, even something as simple as having a cup of tea together. Hanging on the wall of our family room is a picture of a tea kettle and some tea cups. The picture was an anniversary gift from me to Maureen. I wrote on the back of it: "For my beloved wife on our 13th anniversary—I'll always treasure our times of tea together. Love, Lanny." Some years earlier, we had an argument. When I had left the house to cool off, I ended up purchasing a set of tea mugs as a symbol of our solidarity. Sharing a cup of tea together has been our daily activity—in good times and bad—throughout our twenty years of marriage. It sounds so easy and natural, but sometimes we need to pay attention to taking time together doing the special and ordinary things that draw us together.

WE   CANNOT   REALLY   LOVE
ANYBODY WITH WHOM WE NEVER
LAUGH.

Agnes Repplier

Meet and Do Things Together

- Discuss the following questions with your spouse related to the time you spend with one another:

  How much time do we spend together during an average week?

  What are some things that we like to do together?

  How often do we do these things?

  How can we find more time to spend together?

- Play a favorite board or card game together.

- At least two days each week, take a thirty-minute walk together.

- Think back to some simple pleasures you and your partner enjoyed doing early in your relationship. Try doing them again now.

- Charlotte and Howard Clinebell note that couples can nourish their relationship by nurturing the many kinds of intimacy in marriage: "There are more areas in which creative closeness can grow than most couples even suspect. . . ." Reflect on more of the Clinebells' ideas:

    Emotional intimacy is the depth awareness and sharing of significant meanings and feelings. Do you share emotional intimacy?

    Intellectual intimacy is closeness resulting from sharing the world of ideas. Do we ever talk about our ideas, what we're thinking about or reading?

    Aesthetic intimacy is the deep sharing of experiences of beauty. Do we see movies, plays, or concerts together? Do we ever sit together and gaze at a spectacular sunset?

    Creative intimacy is the intimacy of shared creativity. Do we make new things together: start a new garden, put up new wallpaper, and canoe a new river?

    Recreational intimacy is essential to the mental health of the partners, refilling the wells of energy and allowing one's "child side" to rejuvenate the personality through stress-relieving play. Have we developed any new recreation together: walking, biking, fishing, working out, or golfing?

    Work intimacy is the closeness which comes from sharing in a broad range of common tasks involved in maintaining a house, raising a family, earning a living, and participating in community projects. Do we have at least one common activity that falls under work intimacy?

    Spiritual intimacy is the nearness that develops through sharing in the area of ultimate concerns, the meanings of life, their relationship to the universe and to God. How often do our spiritual lives converge and grow together?

MARRIED LOVE IS NOT A STOLEN,
ISOLATED PART OF LIFE; BECAUSE IT
IS INTEGRAL TO ALL OF LIFE'S
INTERESTS, IT BRIGHTENS NOT
MERELY A CORNER, BUT LIFE ITSELF.

Dwight Hervey Small

Our Special Box of Letters

Maureen and I have been married over twenty years and one of the most precious possessions we have is a large box of letters that we exchanged from 1976 to 1980. In that four-year period we only talked by phone one time but, through our letters, we found each other.

Maureen is from Dublin, Ireland, and I am from Minneapolis, Minnesota. Since my grandfather was born in Ireland, I went to visit this beautiful country in the summer of 1976. Through some mutual friends, Maureen and I met at a volleyball party on a Dublin beach.

I remember feeling nervous when I telephoned her to see if she would go out with me. I also remember the frequent bus trips from downtown Dublin up to Maureen's home on the north side of the city. During the summer we did a lot together: plays and movies, rides on the bus, walks, and as is customary in Ireland, we would drink tea together in small cafés. While we enjoyed each other's company, we never talked much about our feelings for each other.

When I returned to the United States at end of the summer neither of us knew if we would ever see each other again. We exchanged a few letters for a couple of months, but then our communication ended.

Two years later, I sent Maureen a birthday card. When she wrote back, she indicated that she had plans to visit an American family in Florida during that coming December.

I flew down to Florida to see her for one day. As I drove into the neighborhood where Maureen was staying, excitement and nervousness swirled inside me. I hoped she might still be interested in me.

I picked her up, and we went down to the ocean a few blocks away and had a long talk about what we each had been doing the past two years. Although it was obvious we cared for one another, we were too reserved to let each other know our hearts' desires. After several hours together, it was time to say goodbye. We embraced. It was the hardest and most confusing goodbye of my life.

I had seen Maureen, but did not communicate my deep feelings for her. As I drove away, I felt a profound emptiness. Soon she would be back in Europe. She was gone. Maybe forever.

But something bigger than I first realized did happen that day! We had connected with each other after two years apart. We walked along the beach, ate together, talked all day, and watched the ocean waves. We embraced one another as we parted. In our brief meeting, together our lives became closer.

In the next eighteen months our relationship grew more deeply through shared letters. We began opening up about what was going on our lives, and eventually our interest in one another. In the fall of 1979, Maureen attended college in Paris, France, and I was in Chicago at school. We longed to hear from one another and enjoyed getting the letters. I still remember the day I received a collection of pictures that Maureen had sent. I framed them and would look at them each day. We were falling more deeply in love.

As the months went by, however, something was missing: *meeting together to do things!* One day a friend of Maureen's from Paris visited Chicago, and we met and talked together about Maureen. This woman shared things about Maureen, such as how she would smile, laugh, and act. It was during that conversation that I realized I had forgotten how Maureen acted in these ordinary ways. I knew many deep facets of Maureen that this friend did not know, but there were the everyday types of behaviors that I had forgotten. In our letters during the winter, we made plans to meet again in Ireland during the summer.

Throughout the summer of 1980 we immersed ourselves in each other's lives. We talked for hours, rode the bus all over Dublin, visited stores and museums, and went to parties together. While we had shared many important things by mail, we were both reserved as we approached each other in person.

As the weeks passed, and knowing our time was limited, we felt some pressure to decide what we wanted to do regarding our relationship. One day we traveled by train to Donegal, a beautiful town in northwest Ireland. Walking along the ocean beach, we talked about our relationship, but tiptoed around whether to move our relationship to a deeper commitment. And then it started raining. Walking along in the dreary wetness, silence lingered between us. We felt awful.

As we took shelter in a café throughout the afternoon, we drank tea. Little by little, word by word, we opened up to what truly existed between us. Pots of tea later, we knew that our relationship was meant to be a lasting one. Soon thereafter, we were engaged to be married. I had to go back to the United States to start school in New York. We would again be apart for the four long months until our marriage. In the days leading up to saying good-bye, Maureen would grow tearful whenever the separation came up. I contained my emotions pretty well until we reached the Dublin Airport. As the time came for me to board the plane, I began weeping. Just as we had shared our tea and walked on the beach together, now we cried together. But as I walked to the plane I knew that this good-bye did not have an uncertain future. We knew we would soon be together to do all those simple things that brought us to love each other from the beginning.

LET US CONSIDER HOW TO PROVOKE ONE ANOTHER TO LOVE . . . , NOT NEGLECTING TO MEET TOGETHER, AS IS THE HABIT OF SOME, BUT ENCOURAGING ONE ANOTHER.

Paul of Tarsus

Busy Signal

Roger and his partner opened a restaurant right in the heart of downtown where business deals are made over dinner and drinks. The restaurant was successful and received an excellent review in the city magazine. Roger admitted that he is a workaholic, but he added that his hard work had paid off. "I grew up with nothing, watching my dad sweat his way to retirement. Then he collapsed with a heart attack nine months after he retired." Tears sprang to his eyes as he wrung his hands. Roger's expensive suit could not conceal his own sweat.

Jessica worked equally hard at her job as an attorney. Even after long hours at the office, she frequently brought work home at night and on weekends. Jessica never really knew her own father except through stories. He had left when she was four years old. He had struggled with alcoholism, and two years ago she learned that he had died homeless in California. Her mother had to go on welfare to support Jessica and her sister. Jessica indicated that she now loved to give her mother the things she could never have when growing up. "It took a great deal of hard work for me to get where I am today. Even though I am successful it is still hard for me to shake off my childhood spent in poverty." As Jessica shared this, Roger was captivated by her honesty. It had been a long time since they shared forgotten truths about their lives.

Roger and Jessica came into therapy because both felt their relationship lacked some essential ingredient. They complained that they were not spending enough time with each other. They avoided being in the same room at home, looked for ways to schedule things in order to be away from the other, and avoided going to bed at the same time. In order to be comfortable spending time with each other, they needed other people around.

Roger and Jessica sat far apart on the couch. I could not help but notice their exquisitely tailored suits, expensive jewelry, and tanned complexions. They both brought in their leather briefcases, daytimers, and cell phones. Their expensive style was in stark contrast to their impoverished backgrounds—and relationship.

As we talked, Jessica remarked, "We used to laugh a lot. I remember back when we looked forward to uninterrupted times together. I guess I'm not sure what has happened to us."

"Success changes things," Roger added somewhat sadly. "Back then, we were poor students shopping at the local thrift stores."

"But wasn't that fun, Roger?" Jessica wondered out loud.

Roger didn't answer. He seemed lost in remembering.

Shaking his head, he said finally, "We didn't know we were changing. I guess it is like cooking lobsters in the restaurant—slowly turn up the heat."

"I think we're well cooked, don't you, Roger!"

At this they both fell silent, shuffling in their seats turning away from each other. A heavy tiredness enveloped the room, and I saw glimpses of how tense and defeated they were in their relationship.

One thing that Roger and Jessica agreed on was that they rarely fought. Jessica joked that this was because they didn't have any conversations. When they did talk on their cell phones, their conversations were limited to their schedules, why one would be home late, who was picking up the laundry, and who would take the dog to the veterinarian. Once home, both were exhausted. Roger usually hopped on the computer and e-mailed friends for a couple of hours. Jessica got on the treadmill and then took a hot bath before bed. Jessica was asleep by 10:00, while Roger unwound watching the sports channel until midnight. This had been their routine for the last couple of years.

Their relationship slowly evolved into a predictable routine. Their life together was comfortable, but also dry, boring, and empty. I had the feeling I was talking to roommates, not lovers. They had taken their relationship for granted, believing that their love was strong enough to withstand long stretches of time without fully interacting with each other.

When I brought up the concept of doing things together, they protested that they were too exhausted to go out. Roger grumbled that the last place he wished to meet in was a restaurant, and Jessica wanted to avoid people after being in a crowded office or court house most days. However, like true problem solvers, they became intrigued with the idea of doing things together at home and later perhaps coming up with things to do together outside of home.

We began to brainstorm on ways they could reduce their weekly schedules. Both concurred that they could shave time off the work hours. Jessica wanted to learn to leave work at the office and be more emotionally present at home. Roger would request his business partner take over some weekend shifts. Jessica asked Roger to reduce his computer time, so he scheduled an hour for it instead of two. Jessica decided to do her workout earlier and that freed her up to talk with Roger when he got off the computer.

Old habits die hard, but eventually Roger and Jessica became skilled at not bringing their work home. They reported that they enjoyed spending more time together. When issues did come up, they were able to work through them. Most nights they jealously guarded their time together. They began to do things like working together on a project, taking their dog for walks, or just sitting by the fireplace or together on the deck. They gradually recovered the sense of adventure that they had enjoyed in each other in the first place.

I HAD WALKED INTO MARRIAGE EXPECTING A FINISHED HOUSE. INSTEAD, I FOUND THAT MUCH BUILDING NEEDED TO BE DONE; WE WERE ONLY GIVEN THE SHELL.

Philip Yancey

WAY 2 :

Accept the Similarities and Differences in Each Other

MARRYING A MAN IS LIKE BUYING
SOMETHING YOU'VE BEEN ADMIRING
FOR A LONG TIME IN A SHOP
WINDOW. YOU MAY LOVE IT WHEN
YOU GET IT HOME, BUT IT DOESN'T
ALWAYS GO WITH EVERYTHING IN
THE HOUSE.

Jean Kerr

Sociologist Richard Klemer relates these words of Eloise and John, a married couple he knows:

Eloise:

John is ruining our marriage! I work hours preparing a nice dinner for him, and he's never on time to eat it. The worst part about it is that he doesn't even call me to let me know that he'll be late. He wasn't that way before we were married.

I'm tired of begging him, and I'm tired of screaming at him.

John:

Before we were married, she didn't give me the stuff she does now about her father always being on time. She and that perfect father of hers. He had a nine-to-five job and was never a minute late getting to the office and never a minute late getting home. I feel like such a baby when I have to report to her every five minutes.

John believes it is proper for him to come home late when his job keeps him overtime. When he worked overtime before his marriage, his mother wouldn't criticize him. Now he cannot understand why his wife refuses to serve him dinner when he comes home late. Eloise expects John to be home on time for dinner like her father always had been.

Like John and Eloise, all of us bring to marriage certain views, traditions, and prejudices with respect to certain areas in the marriage relationship. However, just because spouses hold different beliefs does not mean that they cannot work out solutions satisfactory to each of them. Rather, problems usually come when two people are unable or unwilling to understand each other's thoughts and feelings.

Accepting one another's differences and adjusting to them is fundamental in building a healthy relationship. Before they are married, two people have lived separate lives for maybe twenty or thirty years. They have formed personal habits and values. Once married, they live together, eat together, sleep together, and give themselves to each other. They begin to unveil their bodies, their minds, and their deepest ambitions. Early in the relationship they might not think of this as an invasion of their privacy. Their strong desire for each other draws them together, and they sacrifice many of their own personal desires in order for the relationship to run smoothly. A kind of merging comes out of the mutual loving. As trust grows, husband and wife gradually become less guarded about their differences. Their inadequacies as individuals become more apparent to each other. They have grown up in different families and different neighborhoods. It is possible that they came from different societal classes, different states, and maybe even different countries. They might have been exposed to different schools, religions, philosophies, cultures, and political views. As a result, misunderstandings, disagreements, and adjustments are to be expected.

When I fell in love with Maureen, I did not realize how different we were with respect to hobbies and recreation. While I remember going to sporting events as a child with my family, Maureen remembers being taken to museums and art galleries with her family. If we are vacationing in another city, she is interested in where the museums are, and I look for the ballparks. While watching television, Maureen will enjoy documentaries on science and history, and I will enjoy sports.

While respecting these differences, we have each supported the other's interests. In our twenty years together I have grown in my enjoyment of museums, art, and documentaries, but recognize that Maureen will probably always have a deeper appreciation of these. In a similar way, Maureen has accepted my love of sports and has periodically joined me at sporting events. As a gift to me she even attended a football game on our tenth anniversary.

In accepting each other's differences, we have also noticed our similarities. We both enjoy British comedies, reading, spirituality, movies, and the social sciences. Since we are both mental health therapists, we also share many common interests in our chosen profession.

All of us are unique. When two people are joined together it is natural that they will more easily unite around their similarities. Their differences can be divisive. However, when people accept each other, their differences can enrich the relationship.

IT TAKES TWO TO MAKE A MARRIAGE A SUCCESS AND ONLY ONE A FAILURE.

Herbert Louis

Accept the Similarities and Differences in Each Other

- Talk with each other about how you are similar and different in the following areas:
    gender
    personality
    values, beliefs, and ethical habits
    family of origin and culture
    socioeconomic level
    educational levels
    religion
    hobbies and recreational activities
- Take turns relating how you personally experienced an important event that you shared together.

- Create a picture; start by drawing two large overlapping circles. Where the circle overlaps write the word "WE" and then list those items that symbolize your similarities. Then take the two parts of the circles that do not overlap and place write "I" and then list those items that symbolizes your individuality.

- In light of the values and beliefs you were raised with, how do you handle accepting each other, especially in your differences?

- In what ways do you accept the other?

ACCEPTANCE COMES EASIER WHEN YOU DON'T EXPECT PERFECTION OF YOUR MATE. AND IT HELPS TO KEEP THE BIG PICTURE OF ALL YOUR MATE'S GOOD QUALITIES IN VIEW.

Annie and Steve Chapman

The Death of Our Son

In August, 1987, we were awaiting the birth of our third child. We already had two beautiful girls. Erin was five, and Christine was two and a half. For some reason, with this pregnancy, I was a little more anxious and would frequently ask my physician for reassurance that everything was okay. Even with the ultrasound showing a healthy baby, I kept having premonitions of impending doom. I attributed this to my Celtic superstition.

The day I went into labor, when my contractions had barely begun, I attended the funeral of an elderly man Lanny and I had become acquainted with. As I stood by this man's coffin gazing at his lifeless body, my soon-to-be-born baby kicked furiously as if to protest his pending birth. Touching the cold hand of the dear old man and simultaneously feeling the strong kicking of my baby, I pondered the life-death cycle and how fragile we really are, especially when we are at the extreme ends of life, infancy and old age.

During my pregnancy, Lanny was in a busy time of his career. As much as possible, he tried to be involved with the pregnancy and to connect with the baby. When I went to the hospital later that night, he was excited and attentive to me, even though he was fighting physical exhaustion.

Low lights, classical music, and a calm medical staff aided my labor. I was even fortunate to have my regular doctor on call for the delivery. Quietly—as if not wanting to break the serene moment—our baby boy, Sean, slipped into the world. He looked like a wet little bird holding his wings together tightly in the rain. We welcomed him fondly, kissing his red scrunched-up nose. We instantly fell in love with our little man.

Strange for a newborn, Sean hardly seemed to sleep. His coal black eyes appeared to take in everything, so much so that Lanny commented, "He seems like a little tourist, taking in all the sights!" Little did we know that Sean would be going back home soon after his brief visit to us.

When Sean was just a few days old he became desperately ill. The doctors discovered that he had a life-threatening heart defect and without a heart transplant he would quickly die. With no infant heart available, Sean became too weak for surgery, and we were told that there was nothing anyone could do for him. He fought hard to live, and we stood beside him in the dead of night. We were able to hold him until he passed from this world to the next and then to spend time together with the lifeless body for as long as we desired.

At about three in the morning, we gathered our things together at the hospital and drove home as grief-stricken parents—an empty baby car seat sat in the back seat. Beginning the next day, visitors started flowing over to our home. We cried together with friends and family. Visiting the funeral home, we had to pick out a casket. Then we could go to privately view our son's body.

Both Lanny and I were grieving deeply in these opening days of our loss. A couple of days later we had a memorial service, and Lanny carried Sean forward in a little casket. On the tombstone we had the words cast, "Into the Hands of God."

To say that we were devastated by the loss of our beautiful baby boy would not adequately describe the depth of our despair. Telling Sean's sisters that he wasn't coming home was heartbreaking. They couldn't comprehend why he was gone. Nor could we. Seeing his empty crib, newly decorated nursery, and feeling milk leak from my breasts was almost too much to bear. That the world still turned amazed me because my world had crashed around me.

Soon after Sean's funeral a deep depression descended upon me. My grief had enveloped me, and I couldn't find my way out. Lanny had to become mom and dad to the girls and try to work his demanding job. My milk eventually dried up, but my tears flowed spontaneously and continually. But Lanny hardly seemed to cry after the first couple of weeks. I was puzzled over this and soon my puzzlement turned to anger. "Why is he not hurting like I am?" I would ask myself frequently.

I found comfort going to Sean's grave on a regular basis, but Lanny did not have that strong pull like I did. My arms were so empty for my baby they ached. I couldn't sleep at night, but Lanny had no trouble falling into a deep and heavy slumber.

In my own pain, I compared what I thought were the differences in our grief. I came to feel that how I experienced Sean's death was the only true way to grieve for our child. I assumed that just because Lanny's tears did not flow as often, that he could sleep, that he did not visit the grave as often as I did, meant that he was not grieving. I even went so far as to accuse him of not loving our son as much as I did!

I was so focused on our different ways of experiencing grief that I failed to see the similarities. The similarities were that our hearts were broken, we were both exhausted, we both worried and had become over protective of our two little girls, and we felt guilt over the genetic defect our son was born with.

Gradually through talking out our confusion, our hurts, and our differences, we began to see these similarities. Lanny grieved internally; I expressed it externally. I also realized that he had put some of his grief on hold because he was concerned for me while working and trying to parent the girls when I had little energy. We had to accept where each other was and give permission to each other to experience our differences. I was grateful to Lanny for allowing me to take the time to grieve our son in my own way, and after working through my anger I was able to do the same for him.

We also learned that our differences could be helpful in our time of grief. My longer-lasting grief challenged Lanny to examine his own hurts. Lanny's ability to move on despite his grief encouraged me to find healing and move forward in life.

THE DIFFERENCES THAT ATTRACT PEOPLE TO EACH OTHER IN THE FIRST PLACE MAY BECOME IRRITANTS IN MARRIAGE; DEALING WITH THE DIFFERENCES LEADS BACK TO THE ADMIRATION OF COURTSHIP.

Daniel Lambrides and
Stephen Grunlan

The Flamboyant Artist-Writer and the Conservative Minister

Judy declared that most people would never guess that she was a minister's wife. Her husband was a minister in a conservative Protestant denomination, and she claimed that she did not fit the mold of a conservative minister's wife. Looking at her long, waist-length hair streaked with gray, her long patchwork shirt and the many strands of colorful beads that hung around her neck, I started to see what she meant. Harry's starched white shirt and conservative tie, his pants-legs pressed to a razor sharp crease stood out against the stark contrast of Judy's free-flowing style.

Judy and Harry had met at a writer's conference twenty-five years before. Judy came from the west

coast and Harry from the south. Judy was attracted to
Harry's quiet southern charm. Judy's energy and sense
of discovery intrigued Harry. Harry was brought up in
a strict religious home. Judy's family was not religious,
but they shared a passion for preserving animal rights,
nature, and natural resources. After a short romance
they were married and moved to the east coast so
Harry could finish seminary while Judy taught at a
local Montessori school. The couple visited a variety of
churches, observing different traditions and meeting
new people.

A few months before graduation, Harry began
searching for a church in which to serve. After much
discussion, they decided to stay within Harry's
denomination since Judy had no affiliation with any
denomination. After several months and many
different church interviews, Harry was offered a post in
a church in the south. Two months later Judy and Harry
were unpacking boxes in the small parsonage.

The church had been without a minister for some
time, so Harry had much to do. He quickly jumped into
ministry. Judy's role was less defined. Her role as
minister's wife did not have a job description, and she
had difficulty trying to figure out what she was
supposed to do.

Life eventually took on a regular pattern in this
small southern farming community. However, Harry
and Judy's relationship was also falling into a regular
pattern of conflict. Harry was a natural in his minister's
role. He liked the routine and schedule he kept with
church programs, visitations, and Sunday services.
Judy loved those parts of their lives that involved
caring for people, visiting shut-ins, taking her Sunday
School class of toddlers on nature walks, and hanging
out with the youth group on Friday nights.

However, she hated church business meetings, ladies' teas, and hymn sing-alongs. This was a problem. Harry felt pressure that he and Judy confer with the expectations of the congregation, especially since they were young and this was their first church. They started to argue every day. This all came to a head one weekend when Harry asked Judy to lead the women's retreat that was coming up soon.

Judy refused, and Harry—feeling desperate—flew into a rage. "I can't believe you! You told me that you'd support me in this ministry. You knew what I was all about when you married me. Why can't you just go with the flow? You want me to beg, to plead? Well, I won't. I can't believe your selfishness. I thought you cared about me. Well, I guess I was wrong. It seems to me that you only care about yourself and what is good for Judy."

Judy's blood began to boil as he spilled out rage. So she yelled back. "Well, I can't believe you! You call yourself a minister? The only one you minister to in this marriage is yourself! You brought me down here to this pokey little town, and to think I went willingly. I gave up a lot to follow you into your ministry. And I say 'your' ministry—this is *your* ministry, *your* people, *your* town, and I'm sick to death of all of it. I have had it!"

"Is that so? Well, I guess you know how to fix that, don't you?" Harry continued as Judy stormed into the bedroom.

She pulled out her suitcase and began to throw clothes in. Harry continued raging at Judy. "Oh, that's right, just run. Run on away. Don't worry about me. I'll manage on my own. I've been managing on my own ever since we got here."

Judy stopped packing. Her face was flushed and, when she spoke, her words came out of clenched teeth.

"Oh, that's rich, Harry. Thanks for nothing. I have helped you every way I could, but you can't see that. You are so caught up with being Pastor Harry. You want to look so good to your little congregation that you're willing to sacrifice our marriage. Harry, right now, I hate you!"

Harry marched out of the bedroom, out of the house, and across the street to the church. As Harry sat in the dark sanctuary, he heard a car pull up to the parsonage. He saw Judy putting a suitcase into a taxi, and soon the car sped away. He sat down stunned, staring into space. He knew Judy had been unhappy, but he expected she would slowly adjust. As he thought about it, he realized she had not written any stories for some months now, and he couldn't remember when she had last painted, another of her interests.

He walked back to the empty parsonage and through its silent rooms. He fingered her colored beads, her stack of books, her dried flower arrangements, and he felt suddenly ill inside. The sacrifices Judy had made slowly dawned on him. She had tried hard to enter into a community that was foreign to her, and Harry discovered that night how much he had expected from her.

Judy called that morning from a motel near the airport. Harry asked her to come home, but Judy wanted to take a couple of days to clear her head. Three days later, Judy returned to the parsonage.

While she was gone Judy had contacted a local art gallery that sounded interested in her art, and she also signed a contract with the small town newspaper to write six stories. To Harry, Judy looked more animated and alive than she had been for a long time when she came home.

The next night both Judy and Harry went to the church board meeting and explained that Judy would not be leading the women's retreat and, due to her work schedule with her art and writing, she would not be available on a regular basis for church involvement. There was some grumbling, but Judy and Harry did not waver. They left the meeting arm in arm.

Today, many years later, Harry continues to preach on Sunday mornings. And on those same Sundays, Judy may be in church. Or just as often, she can be found at an art show or volunteering at the local animal shelter.

FREEDOM IN MARRIAGE—YES. BUT IT TAKES UNITY TOO. TOO MUCH FREEDOM ENDS IN SEPARATION AND DIVORCE. TOO MUCH UNITY IS SMOTHERING. HAPPY ARE THOSE WHO FIND IT POSSIBLE TO MAINTAIN A FLEXIBLE BOND BETWEEN GROWING PERSONALITIES. FOR THEM MARRIAGE IS A LIBERATING FORCE AND A CREATIVE ACHIEVEMENT.

Robert Blood

WAY 3 :

Strive to Understand Each Other

COMMUNICATION IS THE LIFEBLOOD
AND HEARTBEAT OF EVERY
RELATIONSHIP. . . . COMMUNICATION
IS THE MOST IMPORTANT OF ALL THE
SOURCES OF HAPPINESS AND HEALTH.
COMMUNICATION IS THE ESSENTIAL
FOUNDATION OF OUR HAPPINESS.

John Powell

People communicate through words and actions and come to a mutual understanding when they listen to the other. Understanding between two people means that they know each other and comprehend what one is communicating to the other.

Disillusionment can begin setting in when spouses recognize that their partner is not completely like they anticipated. The poet Goethe remarked long ago: "Love is an ideal thing, marriage a real thing; a confusion of the real with the ideal never goes unpunished."

Problems can arise because of ignorance, confusion, and disagreement over the expectations that spouses have of each other and of the relationship. A husband discovers that his wife, unlike his mother, is more likely to spend money than save it. The wife discovers that her husband, unlike her family, would rather sleep on mended sheets than purchase new ones. Without communicating they sour towards one another because of attitudes learned but unexamined, judgements made on criteria that lurk unseen, but dangerous.

Partners need to communicate in ways that will help them understand each other. In our own marriage, Maureen and I have often used the "1 to 10" technique to communicate how strongly we feel about certain things. For example: With 1 as low and 10 as high, we each indicate how much we want to go out for dinner. If one says "5" and the other says "7" we can quickly see that one was sort of in the middle while the other would like to go. If one had said "2" and the other had said "9" we would quickly be able to see that one strongly wanted to go out while the other certainly did not. In such a case we would have to dialogue with each other to figure out what to do based upon understanding each other. While this method may not appeal to everyone, it works for us.

One night a few years ago we discovered on short notice that we had a free evening since both of our younger children (who still needed sitting) would be gone that night. On the spur of the moment I had the idea of taking Maureen to a play at a local theater. I asked her on a scale of 1 to 10 how much she would like to go. She said "3"; when she asked me how much I would like to go I said "9" (because I wanted to go a lot). After announcing the number, we each explained some contributing factors to our scores. In this case,

Maureen explained that she would have liked some advance warning since the theater was a place to be dressed up nicely, that if she had more time to get ready her desire to go would have been higher.

Understanding her rationale, I said we did not need to go and could have a quiet evening at home. However, after a few minutes she said, "Let's go." I asked her why she changed her mind. She said that recently I had done some things that she had desired to do even though I had not rated them that highly. As she thought about it she decided it was time to defer to me and join me in something that I had more desire in attending. We got dressed for the theater and had a wonderful evening together.

A decision like this could have been problematic. Perhaps Maureen would have said "no" without explaining, and I could have been upset. She could have said "yes" even though she did not feel like going, but I would never had known that her going would have been a love gift to me because she really did not have a high desire to go. We might have entered a power battle, with me cajoling her into going and her hardening her resolve not to go. By this simple rating, we avoid extremes of "yes" and "no." In this way, we see these issues more clearly and can negotiate the difference.

Non-verbal language needs to be understood too. At times, partners understand each other without exchanging words. If I asked Maureen to go to a play and we were looking at each other, she might have just shook her head indicating "no." If she felt I was pressuring her in an unfair manner, she could have used the "silent treatment" to communicate to me, "Lanny, get lost, there is no way I'm going out with you tonight!" Reaching over to lovingly touch one's partner can say, "I love you." However, actions can be wrongly interpreted, so it's often important to clarify them with words.

Through the use of the "1 to 10" technique, either of us could have raised other questions about going to the theater to give perspective about what to do that evening. "On a scale of 1 to 10, how much do we want to be together tonight?" "On a scale of 1 to 10, how much would we like to have some solitude and do something by ourselves?"

I remember one time we had set aside two days of vacation. After being out the first day together, as we were planning the next day, I said, "On a scale of 1 to 10, I'm about an 8 on needing to have some solitude for part of the day." Maureen volunteered that she was about a "5" regarding solitude for herself. As we talked about it, we decided to have time together and time apart.

The advantage of this "1 to 10" technique is that in a short amount of time we are each able to discern how strongly each of us feels on a particular decision. We also use the 1 to 10 scale for deciding things like who will help with a household task, who will care for the dogs, who will pick up milk and bread, and who will help with homework. This "1 to 10" communication technique can be used for almost anything. Among many tools to ease communication, it is just one. The key here is to find ways that help your talking as a couple, discerning what you both need and want and why.

ONCE   THE   REALIZATION   IS
ACCEPTED THAT EVEN BETWEEN THE
CLOSEST   HUMAN   BEINGS   INFINITE

DISTANCES CONTINUE TO EXIST, A
WONDERFUL LIVING SIDE BY SIDE
CAN GROW UP, IF THEY SUCCEED IN
LOVING THE DISTANCE BETWEEN
THEM WHICH MAKES IT POSSIBLE
FOR EACH TO SEE EACH OTHER
WHOLE AGAINST THE SKY.

Rainer Maria Rilke

Strive to Understand Each Other

- Consider how the "1 to 10" scale could be used to communicate about almost anything within one's marital relationship. For example:

    How much would you like to go to a game?

    How angry are you right now about our relationship?

    How happy are you with how things are going between us?

    How much would you like for us to spend our extra money on a vacation?

    How much would you like for us to save our money instead of spend it?

    How would you like to take the dog out for a walk?

- Practice using the "1 to 10" technique on some recent decisions that the two of you made together. State what the issue was and ask how much on a scale of 1 to 10 you wanted one thing or another.

Listed below are some examples of questions you could use to get started. In each of these questions, take time to come up with your own number first. Then take time to share your numbers with each other and your rationale for selecting that number.

How pleased are you with the way we are using our money?

How satisfied are you with our lovemaking?

How satisfied are you with the amount of time we are spending together?

How happy are you with the way we use our leisure time on our days off and/or on vacations?

How satisfied are you with the amount of time you get to do things by yourself?

How satisfied are you with how we split up the household tasks—does it seem fair?

• Take a walk together and spend some time in silence taking in sights and sounds. Understanding one another can also be communicated while silent.

DIALOGUE IS TO LOVE, WHAT BLOOD IS TO BODY. WHEN THE FLOW OF BLOOD STOPS, THE BODY DIES. WHEN DIALOGUE STOPS, LOVE DIES AND RESENTMENT AND HATE ARE BORN.

Reuel Howe

My Father's Gift to My Mom

I was the eleventh of twelve children in a working class family in Dublin, Ireland. My dad loved to boast that he had half a dozen of each (boys and girls). Trying to feed and clothe twelve children on my father's meager wages was a constant struggle for my parents. We had just two tiny bedrooms in our small red brick, row-attached house. My parents slept on an uncomfortable pullout couch in the parlor (a small room on the first floor), so that the six boys could share one bedroom and the six girls would have the other bedroom. My parents never complained about the hardships. Rather, we would frequently hear them thanking God for twelve strong and happy children.

Although money was tight, we children really never knew how hard up our parents were. Besides the two small bedrooms upstairs and a closet size bathroom, downstairs we had just two other rooms— the small parlor where my parents slept during the night and entertained company during the day, and the kitchen which served as the command post for my mother. There in the kitchen was a large wooden table that dutifully served as a dinner table, homework center, cutting board, sewing table, ironing board, and game table.

The kitchen was always the hub of activity and the warmest area of the house because that was the room where the fireplace was always lit (even in the summer). It was also the place where the radio and television (after 1961) resided, and everyone congregated there for the evening. It still amazes me how my mother got her chores done in that room what with stepping over baby buggies, diapers drying by the fire, twelve children playing and doing homework, my dad trying to hear the latest news on the radio, and of course the dog chewing his bone!

Most of us children, ranging in age from one to twenty, were born at home. When my mother was pregnant with one of my sisters, she developed complications and had to be hospitalized shortly before she was to give birth. She worried about the rest of us children at home and the long hours my dad had to work everyday. The women in our neighborhood rallied together, and all at once we had several "mothers" taking care of us. My father visited my mother every night on the way home from work, and he could see that she needed to be encouraged. He had a plan and began to set it in motion.

His plan was to spruce up our little house before my mother was released from the hospital with her new baby girl. He made his first mistake by telling my mother that "you won't know the place when you see it!" My mother laid awake at night in the dreary hospital ward, thinking of new wallpaper on her kitchen walls or maybe even new linoleum on the floor. She could hardly wait!

Finally the day arrived for mother's homecoming. Children, floors, doors, and dogs were all scrubbed clean, and the children watched out the front window with joyous anticipation for her arrival. When my mother entered our home she gave out a little cry that could not be interpreted. For you see, most of the interior of our little red brick house was now painted battleship gray!

These were the war years and Europe was ablaze. There was no money and even less paint. My dad understood my mother's message, her need for encouragement, and sought a way to give her a boost. He found the only available paint and set to work, all the while thinking of her. To his practical mind, although the color wasn't sunny yellow or charming blue, or happy crimson, it was still new paint, and it was clean. Besides, it would wear like iron!

Although battleship gray would not be her first choice of color or even her hundredth choice, she understood Dad's message of love. He used what was at his disposal to show his love for her. I guess you could say their love shone brightly to brighter gray color walls.

WHEN AN ATMOSPHERE OF TRUST COULD BE CREATED IN WHICH COUPLES COULD SPEAK FREELY WITH EACH OTHER, SOME REMARKABLE CONSEQUENCES FOLLOWED. . . . [EACH COUPLE] STARTED CLEARING UP MISUNDERSTANDINGS, EXPRESSING FEELINGS THEY HAD FORMERLY SUPPRESSED, GETTING INTO HONEST COMMUNICATION WITH EACH OTHER. THE RESULT WAS THAT MARRIAGES THAT HAD BEEN DULL AND SUPERFICIAL CAME TO LIFE AND STARTED TO GROW.

David and Vera Mace

Will You Dance With Me?

Margaret struggled into her second pair of pantyhose. She just ripped another pair trying to pull them up over her ample hips. When she caught sight of herself in the dressing mirror, she stopped tugging at the stockings and slowly sank down on the bed—the pantyhose digging into her thighs. Her face was flushed from all her efforts to look nice.

"Who am I kidding?" she asked the woman in the mirror. She looked at her white flesh spilling out over her bra and panties, and slowly rolled the stockings back down to her ankles.

Denny called from the shower, "Are you dressed yet, Mag?"

She cheerfully replied, "Yes, in just a minute."

She was always cheerful even when she felt the opposite inside. "Cheery Maggie" her friends called her. Margaret pulled out her usual black stretch pants. "They are very forgiving," the sales lady in the Plus Size Women's store had said. She pulled out a large black shirt. "Covers a multitude of sins" the same saleslady had said. Margaret thought to herself, "What did it matter anyway what she wore? Denny never notices and he doesn't like me to spend money on foolish stuff." She quickly dressed before Denny came into the bedroom. Several years ago she started to dress and undress in the dark, and Denny didn't seem to care.

Denny quickly got dressed, and they left to go to the club. For years now this was their routine. They would meet their friends (four couples) every Saturday night. They would have a few drinks, eat dinner, and dance a little—that is, everyone danced except Margaret. Denny used to ask her to dance, but she refused.

Eventually he gave up and, when the dancing began, would find an old army buddy up at the bar and talk with him until closing. Margaret watched the couples whirl around the room. She liked to "people watch" and especially to observe the ladies with sequined dresses and how effortlessly they glided across the floor.

Margaret was eating more that weekend, and she knew why. On Monday she had an appointment with her longtime family physician, Dr. Bradley. She liked and respected him, but he always gave her the same lecture. This time it was Margaret who made the appointment because she had not felt well these past few months. Dr. Bradley listened to the symptoms that Margaret had been experiencing. He ran some tests and scheduled Margaret to return the next week.

Before her next appointment Dr. Bradley called her and asked that she come in that same day. Margaret was nervous and asked Denny to go with her. The diagnosis was diabetes. Margaret was devastated. Dr. Bradley gave her medication and diet instructions. He also told her to sign up for a weight management class at the local hospital.

Margaret cried all the way home, and when she got there she climbed into bed and stayed. That night, not wanting to disturb her, Denny slept in the guestroom. In the middle of the night, he awoke to the smell of food being fried. He went out to the kitchen and found Margaret getting ready to eat a large cheeseburger.

The angrier Denny got, the faster Margaret ate. When Denny started to clear the kitchen table, he shook his head in despair. "I don't know what to do with you anymore, Maggie. Didn't you hear anything of what Dr. Bradley told you today? You have got to stop this. What are you trying to do, kill yourself?"

Margaret didn't say anything as she continued to eat the forbidden food. Denny stood there helplessly watching as the food disappeared. "I've had it," he said as he stormed off to the guest room and slammed the door.

Denny got up at sunrise. Margaret was still up. She had cleaned up the kitchen and was sitting in the living room watching the sunrise. As if talking to the sun she said out loud, "I have a problem."

Denny went and sat by her. She didn't look at him while she spilled out all the years of pain that she had endured because of her weight. Before Denny left for work, Margaret made the call to sign up for a weight management class.

That night Denny came home early and brought a gift-wrapped package with him. Margaret hadn't started supper. He handed her a package and said, "Forget supper, we're going out!"

She quickly opened it to find a blue sequined dress just her size. There was a card inside the package that read, "I love you just the way you are, but I want you to be healthy. Love, Denny."

That night they danced for the first time in a long while. Denny went to the classes with Margaret. Now on Saturday nights Margaret is having too much fun dancing to "people watch."

THERE IS ALWAYS HOPE THAT YOUR LIFE CAN CHANGE BECAUSE YOU CAN ALWAYS LEARN NEW THINGS.

Virginia Satir

WAY 4 :

Choose to Feel Each Other's Emotions

EMPATHY ALLOWS [US] . . . TO
SPONTANEOUSLY FEEL WHAT OUR
PARTNER FEELS. EMPATHY MAY NOT
RESULT IN AGREEMENT, BUT IT
ALLOWS US TO DEMONSTRATE
UNDERSTANDING.

Don Dinkmeyer
and Jon Carlson

In any developing marriage, the relationship is deepened when the two people care about each other's feelings. When they open their hearts to each other's feelings they draw closer.

On the drive home from work, Gary was thinking about how he would tell Judy the exciting news that he had just found out he would get the position at work that he had been looking forward to for over a year. However, that afternoon Judy had an argument with her mother and was crying when Gary got home. He asked what was wrong and she told him about another fight with her mother over some unresolved issues they had been struggling with for years.

Many times Gary had listened to Judy talk about her problematic relationship with her mother. But on this evening, what with the good news at work, he just didn't want to listen to her complain again about her mother. He was in the mood to celebrate. Trying to be somewhat sensitive to Judy's hurt he stood there hearing some of her words as he began to look through the pile of mail. Gary was afraid to make eye contact with his wife because he didn't want to sit down for an extended conversation about Judy and her mother. He had good news he wanted to share. He wanted to tell someone!

As he changed into some casual clothes, indecision vexed him. Should he go sit with Judy and feel her pain once more? Or, should he go in and tell her his good news, knowing he would be upset if she couldn't celebrate. He wondered if he shouldn't just avoid any conversation right now.

Gary sat on the edge of their bed, thinking about Judy, their marriage, and calming down. Finally, he sighed, but decided what to do.

"Judy, you go relax on the couch. I'm going to make some fresh coffee, fix a treat, and then we can talk."

Judy's eyes were red, but she tried a smile. When Gary brought in the coffee and snacks, he asked her, "Now what did your mother say this time to get you so discouraged?"

"She said I wasn't very caring because I hadn't called her for two days in a row. I'm so sick of the pressure, guilt, and shame that she throws my way. She's been trying to control me my whole life, even when I left home, and now even while I'm married."

In the past Gary had wanted to fix things by offering solutions. Now he knew better, so he just listened. As the whole mess poured out, Gary reached over and put his arm around Judy. She leaned against him.

Finally, when the last tear had been shed, they sat silently. "Thanks. You're so good to listen again and again, but it always makes me feel better."

Later that night Gary shared his good news. Judy pulled Gary up out of the couch and said, "Let's celebrate. Let's go get the wildest, most fattening dessert they can make!" And they did indeed go off and do just that.

I admired Gary's sensitivity here. A good deal of patience, self-discipline, and sheer love was required, especially since the story of Judy's anguish with her mother was so old. Listening to her pain helped Judy work through her anger. Without the listening, she might have redirected her anger and hurt at Gary or buried it inside where it would fester and poison their relationship.

Like Gary, we are tempted to supply answers. But, like so many problems, Judy has to find the answers in herself. Right then she just needed to catch her breath after blowing off steam. Only then could she listen to Gary. That's the way loving partnerships need to work. After all, maybe next time Judy will be the one with the good news, and Gary will need to get something off his chest. Sometimes the best we can do is just be with our beloved's feelings.

NORMALLY, IT IS ONLY WHEN WE
FEEL SECURE THAT WE DARE TO TAKE
THE RISKS REQUIRED TO INTIMACY.
THE   MORE   ONE   TRUSTS   A
RELATIONSHIP, THE MORE ONE WILL
PROTECT IT AND, SIMULTANEOUSLY,
THE MORE ONE WILL FEEL FREE TO
CHANGE WITHIN IT.

Sidney Hurwitz

Choose to Feel Each Other's Emotions

- Name some of your feelings to which you wish your spouse was more sensitive. Share those feelings with him or her. In turn, ask your partner to do the same with his or her feelings.

- Sit in comfortable chairs. Face each other and make eye contact. Take turns sharing some of your deepest feelings while you look at your partner. If desired, stretch out your hands to one another; hold each other's hands and then take turns expressing those feelings.

- Sometimes feelings are hard to share verbally. In that case, it can be beneficial to write out your feelings. After each of you has written some feelings, take turns reading what the other has written. Respond in writing to your partner.

- Meditate on these words from the Christian Bible: "When others are happy, be happy with them. If they are sad, share their sorrow." When you have finished your silent reflection on the passage, ask yourself: How well do we open our hearts to each other whether happy or sad? Share your responses with one another.

ALL THE PLAYERS IN THE COURTING GAME ARE GUILTY OF A GOOD DEAL OF DISHONESTY AND DECEPTION. . . . THIS MASQUERADE IS CONDUCTED LARGELY OUT OF FEAR THAT ANOTHER PERSON CANNOT LOVE US AS WE REALLY ARE, SO WE MUST TRY TO MAKE OURSELVES INTO WHAT WE THINK THE OTHER PERSON WILL LOVE.

Marjorie Casebier and Robert Lee

Changing Dreams

Don and Kathleen lived in a small town in the Midwest. They met at the local lumberyard where they both worked.

Kathleen was raised in a strict Methodist family. Don's leather jacket and shining Harley gave her a glimpse into another world. Don always declared that he was "raised rough." His dad had left his mother and the four boys when Don was just seven years old. His mother cleaned houses to make ends meet and the boys got after-school jobs as soon as they were old enough.

School was not for Don; working with his hands was. So at sixteen he left school, took a job at the lumberyard, and had been there ever since.

After a year of going together Kathleen and Don planned to get married. They wed in a local park. It was simple, fun, and fit the two of them. Kathleen's large, extended family attended, as did Don's mother and brothers with their wives and children. They honeymooned at a friend's lakeside cabin and then settled into a small "fixer-upper" house on the edge of town.

After a couple of years of marriage, their home was neat and very livable. Kathleen had a keen eye for decoration, and Don had put his carpentry skills to good use. Don had surprised Kathleen their first Christmas together with a cute yellow Labrador puppy that she called "Tiffer." Married life was good for them. Don thought maybe a little too good as he would pat his round tummy. Kathleen was an excellent cook. Only one thing was missing.

On their fifth wedding anniversary, Don took Kathleen to an expensive restaurant. The meal was perfect. Kathleen wore her new dress, and Don wore a tie for the first time since their wedding. But, Don and Kathleen weren't smiling much. They couldn't shake the undercurrent of sadness. Eventually, their talk turned to their desire for a child. They had been trying to conceive for three years with no success. Their siblings all had broods of children. Even an eighteen-year-old niece had had a baby six months ago. Don's co-workers all had children and their insensitive and sometimes crude jokes about his lack of fertility were getting him down.

The next afternoon Kathleen made an appointment with a fertility specialist. Determined to find out what was wrong, they still felt apprehensive about which one of them was having a problem. The final verdict was that they had "unexplained infertility." They were glad for their health, but frustrated by such an inconclusive answer.

They continued to try various treatments over the course of the next year. Their relationship grew tense each month when Kathleen had her period. Tears came readily. They both hid despair inside.

Kathleen had sewn a yellow baby quilt. She called it her "hope quilt." Now she decided to give it to her niece who was expecting her second child. Don had made a little baseball bat and ball rack in his workshop two years previously, and now it sat on a dusty shelf in the garage. Meanwhile they were increasingly curt with each other. They stopped going to the curling club on Saturday nights. Kathleen hadn't gone to her quilting group on Tuesday nights for months, and Don had lost interest in riding with the local motorcycle club.

The day of Kathleen's niece's baby shower, Don watched Kathleen wrap her yellow hope quilt. He stood holding her shaking shoulders, as she buried her sobs into his chest. When she took some deep breaths and wiped away her tears, Don went out to the garage and brought in something wrapped in newspaper. He asked if there was room in the baby quilt box for the baseball rack he had so lovingly worked on. It was Kathleen's turn to hold Don as he sat at the kitchen table, fingering the smooth wood in his big hands.

Later that night at the baby shower the women poured over the variety of baby gifts. "Oohs" and "aahs" rippled between the women and young girls. Kathleen's gift was the last one to be opened. The large box was surprisingly light, but beautifully wrapped. Her niece hurriedly opened up the package and was greeted by lots of tissue paper. She buried her hands into the paper and came up with an envelope. Inside the envelope was a beautiful homemade card with a generous check. There were also homemade coupons for Kathleen's niece to redeem for babysitting by Kathleen and another coupon to be redeemed from Don for doing much-needed repairs at their niece's home. Such generosity brought tears to everyone's eyes.

When Kathleen came home later that night Don had already fixed hot chocolate. They sat down at the kitchen table together smiling at each other. There on the table sat the quilt and baseball rack. And sitting on top was a manila envelope from an adoption agency with the application papers for an adoption.

THE ONLY REAL ARGUMENT FOR MARRIAGE IS THAT IT REMAINS THE BEST METHOD FOR GETTING ACQUAINTED.

Heywood Broun

The Red Shiny Box

Christmas 1944 was a cold one where nine-year-old Frank Junior lived. That December, all he could think about was the train set he had seen in the store window on Main Street. With five younger brothers and sisters, he wasn't sure if Santa could be that generous with his family.

Besides trains, Franky's favorite past-time was to sit out in the garage on a broken stool listening to his dad, Frank Senior, whistle a tune as he worked fixing up cars. They'd sit out there until late at night, with Frank Senior whistling away while Frank Junior tried to solve math problems for his homework. Not much had to be said, it was just good to be in each other's company and away from the commotion of all the younger siblings.

On one of those nights when Franky was getting ready for bed, his dad asked him to go up into the attic to get some old towels he wanted to use as oil rags. When Franky climbed up in the attic something caught his eye: a long red box with a picture of a train set. He examined it, searching every detail of the picture. He could hardly contain his excitement. There were just four more days to Christmas, and he didn't know if he could make it until then.

Christmas Eve followed the usual holiday traditions, but Franky could only focus on that red box in the attic. After a festive dinner, they sang Christmas carols around the piano, and then it was time for bed. Off the children went, anticipation pulling at their sleep.

In the middle of that night Franky was startled awake by his father's frantic shaking. He was immediately engulfed in smoke and started to cough. He tried to follow his dad, but lost him in the thick smoke. A strong arm gripped him and pulled him out of the house. Frank Senior told his son to stay with his younger brothers by the tree in the front yard. Soon his father emerged carrying their mother's limp body. Frank Senior laid her in the snow as he went back in for their two little girls.

Franky shook his mother until she came to. Neighbors ran from their homes to help them. The men tried to enter the home to find Frank Senior and the two little girls, but the flames beat them back. Franky, his mother, and his younger brothers could only watch in horror as the entire home—with Frank Senior and the two girls inside—was engulfed in flames.

Today, many years later, Franky is now a father with a grown son and daughter of his own. On December 7, he and his wife Betty received a phone call that Frank's ninety-year-old mother was failing.

When Frank arrived at his mother's bedside, he gathered his younger brothers around the bed and held their mother just like they had as little boys so many years ago on that snow-covered lawn, watching their world turn to ashes.

Betty could only try to imagine Frank's feelings. His mother had been ill since her stroke ten months previously, but she hung on until the snow started to fly. Then she began a slow descent so that now she was barely breathing. They sat with her until after midnight. Then a few short breaths more, and she was gone.

Betty watched Frank take charge of the funeral arrangements. He comforted his younger brothers while seeing to every detail of the burial. Since the age of nine on that fateful Christmas Eve, he had been used to taking charge.

With the holidays there were the usual festivities. Although Christmas was always a tough time for Frank, he always tried to act happy for the sake of Betty and the kids. Betty suggested that this year they could cut back on visiting relatives, entertaining, and decorating, but Frank wouldn't hear of it. "We have to be there for the kids and the grandkids."

Frank tried his best to get into the holiday spirit, but Betty could tell he was hurting. Like his father, Frank was not a big talker. Nearing Christmas day Betty watched Frank as he became more tired. She caught him frequently staring off into space. She knew that losing his mother had been harder on Frank than he let on. She couldn't get him to talk to her about it, and he hadn't shed a tear. She also felt pretty sure that he was thinking about the loss of his father and sisters. That got Betty thinking.

On Christmas Eve, Betty and Frank had their grown children and grandchildren over for their traditional holiday dinner. After the children had left, Frank told Betty they'd clean up the dishes in the morning because he was too tired to face them that night. Betty told Frank to go on to bed, that she wasn't tired yet and would be up to bed later.

The next morning Frank awoke to a steady snowfall. He lay there remembering Christmases past when his mother would try to boost their spirits. He heard Betty puttering around in the kitchen and smelled the bacon and the coffee. When he came downstairs, she had the radio on, playing Christmas music. She had finished the morning paper. Breakfast wasn't ready yet, so she gave Frank the paper and a cup of coffee. He went to sit in his usual chair in the living room. When he entered the living room, at first he didn't notice what was under the Christmas tree, but then he saw it. His hands shook.

Betty took the coffee cup as Frank slowly walked towards the tree. There he knelt down on both knees. For a long time he just stared at the picture on the box as if he had entered a time warp that brought him back to 1944. He was a nine-year-old boy again, alone, sitting on a cold attic floor staring at his dream come true, a red shiny box with a picture of a train set. He could imagine his father's whistling and the laughter of his little sisters.

Betty put her hand on Frank's shoulder and said, "Open it, Frank." He gingerly opened the faded red box, tears streaming down his face. There, still sealed in its original yellow wrapping, was the train set. Frank stared at it. He ran his fingers over the wrapping, stroking it like he would a baby. He was not yet ready to take it out. It was enough to just look at the picture.

"Where did you find this?" he whispered. Betty explained her hunt over the Internet to find the same make and model of the original train set that Frank had expected to receive before the tragedy.

"I can't give you what you lost, honey, but I want to be there for you." Then she wrapped her arms around him.

At last Frank wept for all his losses and for all his gains. And all he could say through the tears were words of thanks.

"I love you, Frank." Betty wanted to say those words, but she knew deep down that the shiny red box with the train set spoke much more clearly to the man she held and the nine-year-old boy who could now heal too.

A PORTION OF YOUR SOUL HAS

BEEN ENTWINED WITH MINE.

A GENTLE KIND OF

TOGETHERNESS, WHILE

SEPARATELY WE STAND.

AS TWO TREES DEEPLY ROOTED IN

SEPARATE PLOTS OF GROUND,

WHILE THEIR TOPMOST BRANCHES

COME TOGETHER,

FORMING A MIRACLE OF LACE

AGAINST THE HEAVENS.

Janet Miles

WAY 5:

Mindfully Nurture
Your Love

THERE IS NO DIFFICULTY THAT
    ENOUGH LOVE WILL NOT
    CONQUER;
NO DISEASE THAT ENOUGH LOVE
    WILL NOT HEAL;
NO DOOR THAT ENOUGH LOVE
    WILL NOT OPEN;
NO GULF THAT ENOUGH LOVE WILL
    NOT BRIDGE;
NO WALL THAT ENOUGH LOVE WILL
    NOT THROW DOWN;
NO SIN THAT ENOUGH LOVE WILL
    NOT REDEEM.

Emmet Fox

We need love to be healthy or whole. Love is an expression of goodwill towards others. It is the desire of heart, mind, and will to foster the good of others in whatever ways we can and in whatever ways

63

they need. Gerald May says, "To love is to care, to care is to give ourselves, and giving ourselves means being willing to be hurt."

Love serves as the foundation for friendship and marriage. When this kind of love exists within a marriage it nurtures the lives of both the husband and the wife. When we learn to express goodwill to others and to ourselves, when we seek and foster the good of the other, we grow as individuals, as a couple, and we create a new reality: us!

Julie and Jim met each other in a single's club that did a variety of social activities together. When they married five years ago, Julie was in her early thirties and Jim in his mid-thirties. They were both independent and, since neither had previously been in any lengthy romantic relationship, marriage required a lot of adjustments.

While the past two years together have been better, the first three years of marriage were an ongoing battle. They each enjoyed having a companion to share life with, but they found themselves impatient with one another and often critical. As a result, they would bicker and snap at one another. Both wondered if indeed married life was better than single life. They sometimes found themselves nervous around each other and afraid that their actions would produce a negative response from the other, especially around subjects that had turned into running arguments without any resolution.

Jim and Julie argued constantly the week prior to the wedding of two friends. They weren't even sure that they wanted to ride together to the wedding. During the service, the minister praised the positive effects of a marriage relationship based upon the description of love found in the Bible; that love is "patient and kind, not jealous or boastful or proud or rude."

As the minister reminded the listeners, "love is always hopeful, and never gives up, never loses faith, is always hopeful, and endures through every circumstance." While rejoicing in their friends' marriage, sadness at their own marriage threatened to overwhelm them both. They saw how excited their friends were, and they remembered how happy they had been just three years previous.

The day after the wedding Jim and Julie decided that they wanted to make the effort to improve their marriage. The words of the Bible reading on love were printed in the inside cover of the wedding program, and over the weekend Jim and Julie talked at length about how different their relationship could be if they could live according to these words. They made a commitment to try to do so.

Julie and Jim bought a decorative plaque that had these words on it. They hung it in a prominent place at home as a reminder of how they wanted to live. Over the next two years Jim and Julie tried to take each line of the passage to heart.

The first line read, "Love is patient and kind." Jim and Julie tried to be more patient and kind with each other. Perhaps the most challenging line for Jim and Julie was "Love is not irritable, and it keeps no record of when it has been wronged. It is never glad about injustice but rejoices whenever the truth wins out." Arguments and anger will occasionally be part of any relationship and Jim and Julie continued to have their share. The difference was they tried not to record wrongs against the other. Rather than hold things in, stocking up plenty of ammunition, they decided to describe what was bugging them as soon as possible and tell the other how they felt. Now, instead of unloading hoarded blame and stored up rage, they tried to keep to their own truth saying things like: "When you interrupt me, I get upset" instead of "You are so insensitive when you interrupt."

The final statement on the plaque reads, "Love never gives up, never loses faith, is always hopeful, and endures through every circumstance." According to both Julie and Jim, all the conscious effort, the careful tending to their love—based on the biblical passage— has helped their marriage endure. While they have forgiven each other for much of the disharmony of those first three years, they don't forget. Remembering the tough times reminds them to nurture their love— mindfully, consciously.

LOVE CURES PEOPLE, BOTH THE ONES WHO GIVE IT AND THE ONES WHO RECEIVE IT.

Karl Menninger

Mindfully Nurture Your Love

- Make a list of the ways your partner blesses your life. Take time to share these blessings with one another.

- Surprise your partner with a note, card, flowers, or gift just to say "I love you."

- Take time today to compliment your spouse in some way.

- Write about the effect that love has on your relationship. What is it like to live in this relationship when I am feeling loved by you? What is it like to live in this relationship when I am not feeling loved by you? Share your reflections with your spouse.

- Communicating "I love you" can be done in many ways. Ask yourselves in what ways your partner lets you know that you are loved? Share this with each other.

- Like Jim and Julie, talk together about your relationship in light of the same bible passage from 1 Corinthians 13:4-8. How well do you follow these definitions of love?

> Love is patient and kind.
>
> Love is not jealous or boastful or proud or rude.
>
> Love does not demand its own way.
>
> Love is not irritable, and it keeps no record of when it has been wronged. It is never glad about injustice but rejoices whenever the truth wins out.
>
> Love never gives up, never loses faith, is always hopeful, and endures through every circumstance.

LOVE IS THE EXPERIENCE OF KNOWING THAT ANOTHER PERSON CARES—DEEPLY, WARMLY, AND DEPENDABLY: THIS IS THE MOST INDISPENSABLE NEED OF ANY HUMAN BEING TO WHICH ALL THE OTHER HEART-HUNGERS ARE TRIBUTARIES.

Charlotte and Howard Clinebell

Love Keeps My Parents Young

With their two gray heads bent together, one holding a magnifying glass and the other trying to thread the needle, it was hard to tell where one ended and the other began. They even looked like each other.

My father Loren is eighty-five, and my mother Arlene is eighty-six. They have been married for sixty-one years. My parents have had a full life together. They dated as teenagers in their small North Dakota towns, grew to love one another, and were married in 1939. They endured the war years and experienced the insecurities of not knowing where he would be stationed in the military and the times they were apart. After World War II they moved to Minneapolis and raised their four boys. They supported one another's ventures. They welcomed daughters-in-law, grandchildren, and great-grandchildren into their lives. They have been there for their sons when any of us were discouraged, frustrated, or in need. Together they have endured times of sickness, the death of a child, injuries, heartaches, surgeries, and discouragement—but they survived them all with love.

"Love keeps you young," Mom says with a wink. Their life as a couple has been one of small loving gestures strung together in a long chain. It started with him carrying her books to school; now he carries her things because of her arthritic knees. She carried his babies to term and now carries extra batteries for his hearing aid in her purse. For sixty-one years his routine has been to make the coffee while she is in the shower, and she's always allowed him to read the cartoons to her over breakfast as they laughed together.

It was very frightening for both of them when she began to experience blurred vision two years ago. They sought medical help and came to find out that she had a deteriorating eye disease. As their youngest son, I remember going with them to the eye specialist when he explained the laser procedure he would try in hopes of saving her vision.

Instead my mother rapidly lost much of her eyesight and is now considered legally blind. On that fateful day when they returned home from the eye clinic with the news of her serious eye disease, my mom went into the kitchen to make supper. My dad watched her feel her way around the kitchen, as she tried to read can labels with her magnifying glass. He realized then what he had to do. He came behind her and untied her apron and asked her to sit down and rest.

She watched her husband cook the meal, something she typically did through the years. She smiled as she saw him produce almost every pot and pan that was in the cupboard. They ate spaghetti that night and, although he complained it was not cooked quite long enough, to my mother it was the best spaghetti she had ever tasted. Dad jokes that "old dogs can learn new tricks" now that he has mastered the grocery shopping and the laundry. With Mom seeing less, Dad reads out loud to her from her devotional book.

Their days have always been filled with meaningful work, helping others, and frequent loving and thoughtful gestures to each other—gestures that at times are unspoken and unexpected, but significant. These daily feedings of their relationship have produced a healthy, thriving, and exciting marriage of two love birds in their eighties.

Even with my mother's poor eyesight and arthritic knees, most days they still walk together on the pathway near their condominium, bending down to pick up trash, feeding the ducks in the nearby lake, and greeting others they meet. Love endures.

WHAT DOES ONE PERSON GIVE TO ANOTHER? HE GIVES OF HIMSELF, OF THE MOST PRECIOUS HE HAS, HE GIVES OF HIS LIFE.

Erich Fromm

A Change of Heart

Liz didn't see it as a loving act as she washed her husband's body down while he laid on his back in bed. She had become an expert in rolling Ron from side to side while not disturbing his back brace.

Their twelve-year-old son, James, hovered at the foot of their bed with the morning newspaper and a cup of coffee for his dad. He asked the same question he asked every morning, "How ya' doing, Dad?"

His father replied, "Oh, just great son," not sounding too convincing.

After Liz hustled out James and the two girls—Cora and Marie—to the school bus, she went back into the kitchen. She had been up for two hours already and hadn't had a cup of coffee yet. Just as she poured out a cup Ron called from the bedroom for the bedpan. By the time she got back out to the kitchen her coffee was lukewarm.

After just a sip she poured it out and began to load the dishwasher. She stood and watched the rain dash against the kitchen window and gasped because she had hung some laundry outside to dry on the fence because their dryer was broken.

She had to go through the cluttered garage to get to the backyard. Ever since the accident she hated going through the garage. She maneuvered her pregnant body between Ron's two snowmobiles. She stopped at the front of one of them, running her hand over the twisted metal. She started to feel nauseous and quickly went to the bathroom. Ron called for the bedpan again.

Four months earlier, Ron and James had taken the two snowmobiles out for a ride after a heavy snowfall. When the police came to the door, they told her that Ron's snowmobile had plowed into a tree and he was badly injured. A severe back injury coupled with broken bones in his leg had laid him up ever since.

After the initial shock and relief wore off, Liz had to deal with her anger. Anger at Ron for his selfishness in pursuit of his hobbies and anger at herself for how she would passively stand by while Ron bought new outdoor toys or was packing again to go on another adventure. Before they had children, Liz loved to do some of these activities with Ron. But, now, well . . . having a dryer that worked was much more important than having two new snowmobiles.

A couple of weeks later, Ron was able to move to a chair in the living room. Liz decided the time had come to have that conversation with him about her feelings.

"Ron, I've got to say all this or go nuts." When he started to interrupt, she said, "No, honey, don't stop me. I've got to get this out all at once or I'll never say it. Please." He nodded. His eyes never left hers, now filling with tears.

"I love you, but I'm so angry it hurts. I loved all those times we had camping and fishing, but things are different. I'm having a hard time managing. The dryer's broken. The house badly needs repairs. I resent those damned shiny machines sitting out in the garage while I have to stomp out in the snow to hang up freezing laundry. And now this. We haven't gone to a movie together. The girls seldom see you on weekends. I want to see you more and spend more time with you, but snowmobiles and pregnant women don't mix."

She stopped. Ron's face contorted with anger and hurt. He stared at her silently. "Think about it, Ron. I'd like to have you around for our kids, all our kids." Liz got up quickly and made it into the kitchen before breaking down in stifled sobs.

Two weeks went by and on an early Saturday morning Liz heard a knock on the front door. On the front porch stood four of Ron's fishing buddies. She started to tell them about Ron still being laid up when she noticed that instead of holding their usual fishing gear they had hammers, saws, nails, and a bunch of other work tools. They entered the house, winked at Ron as he sat propped up in the living room, and he produced a "to do list" from his pocket. They proceeded to fan out all over the house.

As they started their work, the door bell rang again. In marched their wives, bringing meals for the family to store in the freezer.

"What's going on, Ron? How did you organize all of this?" Ron pulled Liz down beside him and held her.

"I'm sorry, Liz, your words hit me hard a couple of weeks ago, and I was pretty angry. Now I realize how selfish I've been with my time and with our money. I never meant for you to do without. It's just that I got caught up in my own stuff. Will you forgive me?" She answered him with a hug and a kiss.

LOVE IS THE ONLY GAME THAT IS
NOT CALLED ON ACCOUNT OF
DARKNESS.

M. Hirschfield

WAY 6 :

Make Your Relationship Priority Number One

EVERY MARRIED COUPLE BELONGS
TO THREE FAMILIES. THEY BELONG
FIRST OF ALL TO THEMSELVES. THEY
ARE THE "WE" OF THE NEW FAMILY
THEY ARE FOUNDING TOGETHER.
BUT, AT THE SAME TIME THEY
BELONG ALSO TO "HIS" FAMILY, AND
TO "HERS." IF THEY ARE TO
ESTABLISH A STRONG FAMILY UNIT
OF THEIR OWN, THEY MUST
INEVITABLY REALIGN THEIR
LOYALTIES TO THE PLACE WHERE
"OUR" FAMILY COMES BEFORE
EITHER "YOURS" OR "MINE."

Evelyn Duvall and Reuben Hill

Gretchen and Craig have been married for twelve years and for the most part have been happy together, especially during the first few years of marriage. They are in their thirties and have two children, ages eight and six. They have found themselves arguing more often and sometimes resenting the relationships that each have with other people.

Gretchen comes from a tight-knit family from a small town in western Minnesota. She has stayed close to her family. Craig's family gets together for holidays, birthdays, and during the summer months at the family cabin. He works in the small family business with his older brother. His parents own the business and at times try to control Craig, especially while he is at work.

Early in the marriage Gretchen and Craig were so in love that they enjoyed nothing more than spending time together. Their marital partnership was placed ahead of their parents, siblings, friends, and co-workers. They knew that they gave each other priority over other human relationships. They came home from work looking forward to hearing about each other's day.

But holiday and vacation times were always stressful. They enjoyed being by themselves and with friends, but both of their families wanted them back for holidays, and both families had summer cabins where the grown children would come. While Gretchen and Craig love their folks and siblings, the push and pull from both families had begun to cause tension.

In the first couple years of marriage Gretchen and Craig typically visited each other's family cabins two to three times over the summer, but on some weekends did activities with other friends instead.

After the first child was born Gretchen cut back to half-time at her work. With the arrival of their second child, she quit working outside of the home altogether. Craig increased his hours at his job to replace the lost income. With Craig working more and with the demands of young children, they had less time together. With the loss of some work relationships, Gretchen began reconnecting more closely to her parents and siblings.

Since Gretchen's sister also had small children and was living in Minneapolis, they would talk on the phone and get together two to three times each week. Sometimes their mother would come to the Twin Cities and spend time with her daughters and grandchildren.

Craig began to spend more time with his older brother and father. They would go out for drinks after work and would hunt together in the fall and fish in the spring and summer months. He started wanting to spend more weekends at his parent's cabin. When he went with Gretchen to visit her family, she went off with her sister and mother and he consequently didn't enjoy himself as much.

Gretchen, on the other hand, wanted to go to her parent's cabin on the weekends and didn't want to go to her in-law's cabin. She noticed that when she went with Craig to visit his family, he would go off with his father and brother. She didn't enjoy herself as much as before either.

Almost imperceptibly, Gretchen and Craig had ceased making their relationship central. Other relationships filled the time and space they needed for each other.

As we talked about what was happening, they realized that they needed to again find tangible ways to reinforce their companionship each week. They hoped that in doing so their resentment towards each other's families would subside. As hard as it seemed to them, they knew that they need to put their relationship in first place. To nurture their marriage, they needed to put it before parents, friends, and work relationships.

The biblical passage about marriage—"a person leaves one's father and mother and is joined to one's spouse"—indicates the sort of loyalty to one's marital partner that must stand above even one's family of origin.

WHAT REALLY MATTERS IS THAT YOU NEVER LET YOUR SPOUSE FORGET THAT YOU ARE DEVOTED TO THEM.

Lois Liederman Davitz and
Joel R. Davitz

Make Your Relationship Priority Number One

- Take stock of the clutter in your life. Clutter can be too many possessions, too many activities, too many worries, too many "have-to's," too many people. Write down at least some of that clutter that you are willing to eliminate because it tends to get in the way of your commitment to your partner. Plan to do this exercise every six months. Watch out that you don't replace the eliminated clutter with new clutter.

- Make a list of the important relationships you have in life (children, parents, good friends, work associates, etc.). On a scale of one to ten (1=low commitment and loyalty; 10=high commitment and loyalty), put a number next to each individual's name. Note the highest scores and see if these relationships sometimes threaten the priority of your marital partner. Share and compare your list with your spouse.

- Look at your marriage relationship and consider some situations when you know you placed your loyalty to another human relationship above your marriage. What happened? How did this affect how you viewed your partner? How did it affect your partner?

- Do the previous exercise from the other's perspective: Consider some situations when you suspect your spouse placed his or her loyalty to another human relationship above your marriage? How did it affect how your spouse viewed you? How did it affect you?

- As a sign of giving your relationship highest priority, plan something important together and follow through on doing it: for example, a trip, a vacation, a remodeling project, planting a tree.

PEOPLE GROW TIRED OF MARRIAGE, SOME PEOPLE DO, BUT ONE IS NEVER BORED WITH A COMPANION WHO SEES THE WORLD THROUGH THE SAME RIDICULOUS DISTORTING LENSES THAT WE LOOK THROUGH OURSELVES.

Frank Case

My Father's Funeral

In 1993, my father suddenly and unexpectedly collapsed on the kitchen floor and died instantly of a heart attack at the age of eighty-two. Funny to say, but it was the type of death he prayed for, no lingering in pain or long good-byes. For us he was gone in an instant, but mourned forever.

Flying back to Ireland from the United States for his funeral was the saddest and loneliest journey I've ever had to make. Dad had always met me at the airport wearing his familiar brown corduroy hat with the green feather on the side. His beaming smile was like a beacon in a sea of faces at the airport.

Now with him gone, it gave me comfort as I flew through the clouds watching the sun rise over the green fields of Ireland that Dad was not in pain. I even had a vision of him dying on the kitchen floor. Suddenly he arose and stepped out of his tired, arthritic eighty-two-year-old body and was once again the healthy, athletic, vibrant young man that smiled out at us from the faded photographs on the kitchen wall.

We gathered at his funeral as a clan, children and spouses, grandchildren, and great-grandchildren. It was amazing to see this small army of people generated from one couple. We observed our Irish funeral traditions, which gave us comfort, and at the wake we sang all the old ballads that Dad had sung to us as children falling asleep sitting on his knee. We watched in respectful silence as our elderly mother approached our father's casket. As she held his calloused hard-working hands in hers, we were reminded of how they had made their relationship a priority.

After we arrived home from the cemetery that day, Mother walked through Dad's small flower garden to get to the little red brick house where she and Dad lived for fifty years. She stopped to look at the crocuses popping their heads up out of the soil. These were Dad's favorite. He called them the bravest little flowers, as they were the first to brave the cold spring air. Mother caressed the little flowers before she made her way into the empty house.

After lighting the fire, mother made her way up the narrow staircase to the bedroom where they had slept together for so many years after the children were finally grown and out of the house. She stood in the doorway gazing at the left side of the bed where my dad had slept. The closet door stood open, and there hung his favorite tweed jacket, the one he wore on the day he died. Mother made her way over and took the jacket off the hanger, then held it to her face for a long time. Silent tears streaming from her face, she sank onto the bed where he laid his head. She fingered the leather buttons and the elbow patches and slipped her hands into the pockets. Slowly she spread out the pocket contents on the bed: some coins, a book of matches, a handkerchief, a few receipts.

In the breast pocket lay a yellowed worn sheet of paper that was neatly folded into a tiny square. Mother carefully opened this folded paper. As it unfolded, she could see that Dad's neat flowing handwriting filled the lined page. He had written out his favorite song— the song he sang to her often. As she read the song it was as if he spoke to her from the grave. The day my father died he had a love song, "Silver Threads Among the Gold," in his pocket. It said in part,

> Darling, I am growing old,
> Silver Threads among the Gold,
> Shine upon my brow today,
> Life is fading fast away;

But my darling you will be, will be,
Always young and fair to me,
Yes, my darling you will be,
Always young and fair to me.

We knew that Dad loved us twelve children. But watching my mother murmur the words of this old love song, I knew what we had always known— Mother was first in Dad's heart and mind, spirit, and will. Maybe that's what helped them deal with all that faced them. Without that bond, maybe they could never have loved us so wisely and so well.

"THEREFORE A MAN LEAVES HIS FATHER AND HIS MOTHER AND CLEAVES TO HIS WIFE, AND THEY BECOME ONE FLESH." . . . THE LITERAL SENSE OF THE HEBREW WORD FOR "TO CLEAVE" IS TO STICK TO, TO PASTE, TO BE GLUED TO A PERSON. HUSBAND AND WIFE ARE GLUED TOGETHER LIKE TWO PIECES OF PAPER. . . . [A] CONSEQUENCE OF THIS BEING GLUED TOGETHER IS THAT THE HUSBAND AND WIFE ARE CLOSEST TO EACH OTHER, CLOSER THAN TO ANYTHING ELSE AND TO ANYONE ELSE IN THE WORLD.

Walter Trobisch

Family Ties

Watching the sun rise on a newly planted field was one of the few pleasures that Danny would allow himself. He'd stop on the front porch just long enough to see light stretch across his land and then he'd step off the porch into a fifteen-hour work day on the family farm. This habit was not new; for generations the men and women of Danny's family had greeted the morning by watching the sun rise and would not return home until the sun on their backs went down again.

Mattie, Danny's wife of five years, watched him maneuver the tractor out of the yard as she drank her second cup of coffee. It was another sleepless night. Listening to Danny snore and getting up for the baby didn't help her restless sleep. At night Mattie tried to muffle her crying. It wasn't that she didn't want to disturb Danny, for he slept as deep as any contented person could. It would just hurt more to have him hear the baby's cry and then turn over like he could care less that his wife was also tired and in need of sleep. Mattie was not happy and hadn't been since the first year of their marriage.

Danny and Mattie met in college. She grew up in the city, and he came to the city to attend the university. He majored in agriculture, and they met in a lab class. They hit it off right away. Danny was attracted to Mattie's joy of life, her desire to explore and to experience as much as she could. Danny was attractive to Mattie for his common sense, his value of hard work, his loyalty and commitment to the things he believed in. She was intrigued by his family history.

Danny's ancestors came from Sweden several generations past, and the family has worked the same farm ever since arriving in America. Mattie's father was in the Air Force, and she grew up all over the world, never having a place to call home. Failed marriages and broken family ties tended to give Mattie a sense that her family's history was a crazy quilt.

After dating through college, Mattie and Danny married shortly after graduation. Even though the farming economy had slid into recession and Danny's father phoned him regularly with another dismal report about a neighbor losing his farm, Danny decided to return home to work the farm with his father. Mattie was looking forward to finally putting down roots. After a very brief honeymoon they moved to the original homestead house, situated not too far from the Danny's parents' house.

At the beginning of their marriage Mattie was so busy setting up house that she didn't notice the family dynamics that would later come to really bother her. The men in Danny's family customarily went to the family home for breakfast before going out to the fields. Then at night Danny and his older brothers would return to the family home for their supper before returning to their respective homes, wives, and children. Saturdays were the same as any weekday as far as Danny's routine, and on Sundays Danny would stop over and take his parents to the local coffee shop in town and then go on to church. Sunday lunch was again at his parents' home.

After a few months of this routine Mattie asked her older sisters-in-law about how they handled their husbands' long absences. This question took courage on Mattie's part because she already felt like an outsider with her sisters-in-law. All she got as a reply was "you get used to it."

But Mattie couldn't get used to having Danny at his parents' home every free minute. Even when the weather would get so bad they couldn't go out to do any work, Danny would still leave Mattie to go to visit his parents.

She thought that once the baby came Danny would stay home more. But once Joey started walking, Danny began taking him over there too. Mattie had hoped that her in-laws would baby-sit sometimes, so she and Danny could go to a movie or out to eat. Not so. Danny would give the excuse that he was too tired at night. Her father-in-law would say, "I don't know why you young ones need to go out. Me and Martha never had such luxuries." After a while Mattie stopped asking if they could go out.

For Mattie, loneliness turned to sadness, sadness to hopelessness, and finally depression settled in. She couldn't eat or sleep. The things she once enjoyed didn't interest her anymore. She stopped seeing the few friends she had made in the town, and her motivation and energy to maintain the house was gone. She even went days without showering. Danny would complain about her appearance or the state of the house. They began to argue, and he would typically end up taking Joey to his mom's before he left to go out to the fields.

With Joey now gone during the day, Mattie lost any purpose for getting out of bed, so she didn't. And that was where Mattie's mom, Susan, found her when she came for a visit. Susan had been worried about her daughter for some months. Mattie had quit writing or calling her. When Susan did get Mattie on the phone, she sounded despondent. Susan drove Mattie to the doctor that afternoon, and by nighttime Mattie was admitted to the hospital for her depression.

While in the hospital Mattie waited every day in the visitor's lounge, hoping to see Danny walk through the door. After three days, he did come. He told her the crops had to be taken in, and he couldn't stay long. They sat across from each other not saying much for most of the visit.

Mattie watched Danny watching other people, and she thought about how much easier it would be if she just had to compete with another woman for his attention. She didn't think she stood much of a chance trying to compete with the strong family ties and traditions going back generations.

Danny seemed almost relieved when visiting time was up. He gave her a quick peck on the cheek and was out of the door. He never came back to the hospital.

After her hospital stay Mattie and Joey moved home to stay with her mother. Danny didn't phone her except to say that he had received her letter with the divorce papers. He said he couldn't stay on the line because he was calling on his parents' phone, and he had a lot of work to do. With that conversation, any shred of hope that Danny would try to win her back was gone.

IT IS LOVE THAT ASKS, THAT SEEKS, THAT KNOCKS, THAT FINDS, AND THAT IS FAITHFUL TO WHAT IT FINDS.

Augustine of Hippo

WAY 7:

Delight One Another With Touch

IN A HEALTHY MARRIAGE, SEX IS
AFFIRMED AND ENJOYED SO THAT IT
GIVES THE TOTAL RELATIONSHIP
WARMTH, JOY, AND RESILIENCY. . . .
COUPLES SHOULD BE FREE TO
FOLLOW THEIR OWN IMPULSES
SEXUALLY, TO PLAY AND EXPERIMENT.

Charlotte and Howard Clinebell

Holding, embracing, kissing, and other types of touching are wonderful non-verbal ways of showing love for one's partner. Lovingly holding your partner's hand while on a walk can be incredibly intimate. Leaning up against each other's body or rubbing each other's neck or back while sitting on the couch draw a couple closer. To kiss your spouse on the cheek, forehead, or neck can be a wonderful expression of love. Touching one another with love and delighting each other with touch can be a deeply connecting experience for marital partners.

Avoidance of loving touch can erode a relationship. Couples struggling in their marriage often seem to find touching has become strained and uncomfortable. This was the case for Denny and Jill. In the first few years together, they enjoyed a positive sexual relationship. They each looked forward to the excitement that they would share together in bed. However, in the past year, they discovered that their sexual relationship had declined. Jill had become more resentful of Denny. He had taken on more work and was devoting more time to a hobby he had. During this time Jill began taking on a larger share of household responsibilities, doing more of the things that Denny once did around the house. As they failed to resolve these issues Jill found herself more resentful. Now when Denny would reach out to touch her, she would pull back.

They started looking for excuses to avoid intimate touch. They no longer sat on the couch together to watch television. While they once would go to bed at the same time, now they both looked for ways to avoid each other.

Jill admitted that she'd even pick a fight before bedtime to avoid sex, or she would go off to bed early, saying she was tired. For his part, Denny would fall asleep on the couch or suggest that he slept better elsewhere. As time went on they were kissing less often, holding each other less often, and in general avoiding each other's touch. They sought help because they knew that until they worked through other issues together, lack of sexual intimacy and caring touch would become an additional issue instead of just a symptom.

In other cases, couples may feel emotionally close to one another, but have neglected physical intimacy for one reason or another. Sometimes one or both partners are uncomfortable with sexual intimacy. Sometimes there are unresolved sexual issues in one or both partner's past. Sometimes a couple has enjoyed sexual pleasure, but have attempted physical touch that one or both partners were uncomfortable with and did not communicate this to the other. When these types of things occur, the couple may begin to avoid physical intimacy.

For example, Cathy and Mack were in tears when coming in for their first appointment with me. They loved each other, but had only made love a handful of times in their marriage of four years. A negative sexual encounter in bed early in their marriage had discouraged them from having sex. Periodically, out of guilt, shame, or duty they would try making love again, but typically felt frustrated by the experience. While they enjoyed doing activities and spending time together, any talk about sexual intimacy was avoided. They even avoided holding hands, kissing, or hugging. They felt like failures.

The beginning of their healing came simply by talking together about the problem. Slowly, one touching step at a time, they began reclaiming their physical intimacy.

Many of us—both women and men—have complex feelings about our bodies and about sexuality. Despite all the hype about the sexual revolution, many of us are suspicious of our body and wary of sexual intimacy. Many times we haven't learned the whole variety of ways to touch each other. While we know that sex is not the only type of loving touch, we haven't had much practice in the small intimacies that say "I love you." But we can learn. Delight in touching each other enriches our sense of worth, is empowering, and draws us together closer and closer.

To know another's body and movements so intimately that each moves in harmony with the other as a waltz partner—this is marriage. To lie down together at the end of a day, to stretch however briefly against the loved one while the physical tensions flee before the soft glory of flesh pressed to flesh—this is marriage.

Dorothy T. Samuel

Delight One Another With Touch

- If you have not done so recently, ask your spouse what type of touch they enjoy inside and outside of the bedroom. Make a mental note and touch them the way they like, unless it brings too much discomfort to you. Talk about the type of touch that you do and do not enjoy, too.

- A touch of the partner's hand or arm can be intimate. Giving one's partner a neck or back massage can be an intimate act. Talk about ways that these types of everyday behaviors can be included more often in your relationship.

- Like a dance between two people, it is important to coordinate your sexual intimacy in ways that benefits both you and your spouse. Talk about the sexual intimacy that you share together—before, during, and after sexual intercourse. What are things you wish to modify at each of those times?

• How do your own values and beliefs and those of your partner affect your decisions about physical and sexual intimacy with one another? According to your values and beliefs, are you happy with the physical and sexual intimacy in your lives?

HIS LEFT HAND IS UNDER MY HEAD, AND HIS RIGHT HAND EMBRACES ME. . . . OH, HOW DELIGHTFUL YOU ARE, MY BELOVED; HOW PLEASANT FOR UTTER DELIGHT! . . . KISS ME AGAIN AND AGAIN, FOR YOUR LOVE IS SWEETER THAN WINE. . . . TAKE ME WITH YOU. COME, LET'S RUN! BRING ME INTO YOUR BEDROOM.

Song of Songs

I've Never Stopped Loving You

Darlene reached over to shut off the bathtub faucet. She now waited until the steam covered the bathroom mirror before she disrobed. While waiting, she looked at the silver-lined stretch marks on her stomach. "Love lines," she used to call them. They had been there since she had the first of her four children. Funny how these lines used to bother her so much.

She stood up to disrobe before getting into the tub, and she caught a glimpse of herself in the windowpane. She had forgotten to pull the shade. There gazing back at her was a figure of a woman who looked like she had just emerged from a concentration camp. Her shaved head was white in contrast to her yellowed skin pulled taut over protruding bones. Darlene tried not to look, but her eyes were drawn to the red raw scars on her chest where her breasts used to be. She quickly pulled the shade.

Darlene and her husband Ike didn't look much like the young, smiling couple in their wedding photo. Ike had a middle-age spread from too many executive dinners, and he had lost his flaming red hair before he was thirty-five. Darlene's blond curls fell out after chemotherapy. She now wore a blond wig. Ike and Darlene had a good marriage. They raised their four children. Ike became successful in his career, and Darlene began volunteering in the community when their youngest child started grade school.

Ike and Darlene had always enjoyed their sex life. Sex for them was comfortable, each taking turns to initiate. They valued holding and touching each other outside of the bedroom. Then cancer overshadowed them.

Darlene bravely went through surgery and treatments. But cancer took not only her breasts, it stole her friendship with her body. She stopped initiating sex, and she couldn't bring herself to respond to Ike when he initiated. Even when he would hug her, she'd stiffen. The last time he saw her naked was before her surgery.

After the bath she put her robe back on again. She went into the bedroom and sat on the bed to put salve on her healing scars. She slipped the robe off just as Ike came into the bedroom. Before Darlene could grab her robe, he was by her side. Looking into her eyes, he took the salve from her hands. He bent to kiss her scars and tenderly applied the salve. Tears fell silently from her eyes as he held her gaze. Her body trembled, but then slowly relaxed as they lay back on the bed together.

In one of their later visits with me, Darlene tells us that it was humor that helped them cope with her breast cancer and double mastectomy. As they sit close together on the large couch, their hands entwined, they seem very much in love. Darlene smiles when she quotes Ike's poetry to her, simple rhymes that speak from the heart. Squeezing Ike's hand, she says, "Ike was so patient. I didn't want him to touch me. But he is damned stubborn, and I'm glad now. At least about this. He kept up little touches. Gradually, I could accept that he still loved me, wanted me. It's taken a while, but I think we've enjoyed touch now in more ways than we did even when we were young. And it's so good."

THERE IS INSCRIBED IN THE HUMAN SOUL A LAW OF ALL OR NOTHING IN LOVE. THE GIFT OF ONE'S BODY IS ONLY THE SIGN OF THIS DECISION TO MAKE A COMPLETE GIFT OF SELF WHICH WILL IMPLY ALSO THE MUTUAL GIFT OF ALL ONE'S SECRETS.

Paul Tournier

High School Sweethearts Forever

Bill and Cindy still remember the excitement of kissing each other in an empty high school classroom after school. Each day before after school activities they would sneak off to the basement classroom that was away from most of the activities. They would close the door and find a spot away from the door. They remember wondering if the teachers, students, or custodians in the hallway would walk in.

Shortly after high school, these teen sweethearts married. Bill and Cindy remember their honeymoon when they went off to a deserted cabin for several days. Since neither had much sexual experience before marriage, they had a lot to learn about each other's bodies. They laugh gleefully as Cindy says, "We really got into trial and error!"

One time they were visiting her family for a few weeks in the middle of winter around the first anniversary of their marriage. The old farmhouse had no central heat. To stay warm, they stayed in bed together as long as they could. They recall making love in the squeaky bed as quietly as possible so that no one would hear them. During that visit, their first child was conceived, and by the time they left for home Cindy had morning sickness.

As young children came into their lives they remember the many times that they would embrace each other and wish to be sexually intimate only to have disruptions from the children. There would be a crying baby wishing to fed, so instead of Bill snuggling next to his wife's breasts, his own infants would enjoy them! Or hoping that their preschoolers were asleep, they would quietly have an intimate encounter. Not surprisingly, one of the children would wake up and want a drink or would come and crawl into bed with them. Nevertheless, even when sex was out of the question, Bill and Cindy held each other in bed, two bodies snuggled next to each other.

Cindy and also remembers hearing their children complain—in half-hearted seriousness—that they were getting too mushy. Bill and Cindy would hug in the kitchen and family room and one of the children would somehow sneak between them and get in on some of the affection.

There were also the memories when Bill and Cindy were apart and they would miss each other's intimate touch, days when Bill would travel for work, or they were busy as parents running children in opposite directions. While schedules always seemed full, there were kisses, hugs, neck rubs, and sitting close together on the couch. As they advanced in years they continued to enjoy each other's touch.

After each child was born, they would have to be more creative in their intimacy. And then there were the uncomfortable times when Bill and Cindy were at odds with each other and would avoid touching. But they always made up and forgave each other with words and touches.

Now fifty years after their marriage, they have grown children, grandchildren, and even some great-grandchildren. Neighbors and friends who have known Bill and Cindy have memories of seeing them take their daily walk together. Now that they are each in their seventies, it is not uncommon to see them hand in hand as they walk. They still go to a concert together, arms intertwined.

When Cindy's legs are sore Bill will often massage them for her. Bill himself has struggled with a bad back for years, and Cindy will often rub in some ointment to give him relief. Now wrinkled and gray, they do not have the youthful look of their teen-age grandchildren. But she still sees her handsome Bill, and he still sees his beautiful Cindy.

SEX IS SOMETHING DEEPLY ENJOYED, FREELY GIVEN AND TAKEN, WITH GOOD, DEEP, SOUL-SHAKING CLIMAXES, THE KIND THAT MAKE A WELL-MARRIED COUPLE LOOK AT EACH OTHER FROM TIME TO TIME, AND EITHER WINK, OR GRIN, OR BECOME HUMBLE AT THE REMEMBRANCE OF JOYS PAST AND EXPECTANT OF THOSE YET TO BE ENJOYED.

Sidney M. Jourard

WAY 8 :

Consciously Balance Togetherness and Uniqueness

FINDING THE RIGHT BALANCE
BETWEEN SEPARATENESS AND
TOGETHERNESS IS KEY TO HEALTHY
COUPLE AND FAMILY CLOSENESS. . . .
OF COURSE, SOMETIMES THINGS
WILL GET OUT OF BALANCE, AND
THAT'S OK—AS LONG AS YOU DO
NOT GET STUCK THERE.

David H. Olson and Amy K. Olson

John and Betty had been together for nine years, but had numerous separations in the midst of their tumultuous marriage. Their love for each other had drawn them back together many times, but each time they lived together they had major problems that resulted in another separation.

When together, Betty felt a loss of her independence, seemed to have no voice in their decisions, and always caved in to whatever John wanted. She would get resentful and separate from John. When separated, Betty's sense of individuality would return and, ironically, she and John would spend time together. She would stand up for herself and become more forceful about what she wanted and desired.

Like Betty, each person who gets married faces the task of being a partner without ceasing to be an individual. Many spouses are tempted to put aside their individual desires in order to minimize conflict between them and their partners. They want to get along with their spouses so they emphasize the adjusting, adapting, and agreeing aspects of their personalities. In fact, some spouses set their own interests and needs aside almost entirely. Too often this is what Betty did when living with John. In contrast, a healthy marriage balances individual freedom and commitment to the relationship.

The basic issue is not whether spouses should have *any* freedom versus complete freedom to do as they wish, but rather how to balance individual freedom and joint activities that promote relational growth. A married couple must share a certain number of basic values and key activities. This commonality, however, does not prevent them from going their separate ways at other times. In a healthy marriage individual desires and interests need to be expressed.

When people lose their individuality in marriage they become "fused" in the relationship. According to the *Family Therapy Glossary*, fusion refers to "the tendency of one person to become so emotionally attached to another that one's own sense of self and boundaries become blurred with the other person and an intense interdependency results." Such loss of self indicates that a marriage lacks balance.

Married or not, we need to maintain a healthy sense of our uniqueness. When individuals retain and affirm the "I" in the relationship, they can stand up for themselves. When Betty was separated, she could see herself as an individual who could withstand her partner's pressure. When Betty lived with John, she would not stand up for herself and would lose her sense of identity.

Balancing means that each spouse will pay attention to her or his own interests as well as the interests of the other. Paying attention to what one desires, needs, and is doing, and what one's partner desires, needs, and is doing contributes to a healthy relationship.

An imbalance occurs in a marriage when one person's interests consistently receive priority treatment. Two questions help us seek a balance:

What do I need and desire in my life and in my relationship with you?

What do you need and desire in your life and in your relationship with me?

When one focuses too much on what one needs (question one) there is a tendency to become selfish. When one focuses too much on the other person's needs (question two), there is a tendency to lose one's self. In the latter case, one's own needs and interests can become ignored.

The goal in "balancing" is for the needs and interests of both partners to be considered equally valuable in the marital relationship. After some counseling, Betty and John were trying to be more sensitive to each other's needs. When getting together they learned to speak up for their own personal needs while also asking the other what was needed. John began asking the second question: "Betty, what do you need in your life and marriage to be happy?" Betty began asking the first question more often, "What do I need in my life and marriage to be happy?" As they used these questions, they grew in knowledge and respect for each other. Hope began to blossom again, too.

Sing and dance together and
be joyous, but let each one
of you be alone,
Even as the strings of a lute
are alone though they
quiver with the same music.
And stand together yet not
too near together:
For the pillars of the temple
stand apart,
and the oak tree and the
cypress grow not in each
other's shadow.

Kahlil Gibran

Consciously Balance Togetherness and Uniqueness

- How do you respect your spouse's need for solitude? Does each partner have enough space and time in the relationship? Talk together about each person's need for space and time.

- Good relationships allow for both shared activities and activities done apart. Are each of you taking time for shared activities and activities apart? What are some activities you do together? What are some activities you do apart from each other?

- Reflect and talk about some of the decisions that comprise a marital relationship. Ask yourself: Do I have freedom to make decisions about my own life? Does my partner have freedom to make decisions about his/her own life? Do we work together on decisions that affect both of us?

- In adding up everything that it takes to run our household (e.g., earning wages, paying bills, keeping up the house, vehicle upkeep, caring for children), is there a fair division of responsibility between us? (Another way to check this is to compare how many leisure hours each partner has in a week.)

- In what other areas in our life together is there a balance or an imbalance? Write down these lists and consider sharing your reflections.

MARRIAGE IS NOT A RITUAL OR AN END. IT IS A LONG, INTRICATE, INTIMATE DANCE TOGETHER AND NOTHING MATTERS MORE THAN YOUR OWN SENSE OF BALANCE AND YOUR CHOICE OF PARTNER.

Amy Bloom

Caring and Sharing

David and Kristi are team players in their relationship. They have been married for over twenty years, and he still opens the car door for her. They met when Kristi moved to another state for college. David was an upperclassman and claims their meeting in the library was not love at first sight. In fact, each was dating someone else at the time, which freed them to become good friends.

Kristi was a more social person and preferred cooking good meals and getting together with a group of friends more than studying and writing papers. David was more the studious type and a little less social. They shared their talents with each other, often trading a typed paper for a home-cooked meal, and were mutually satisfied with this arrangement. It seems that this was the foundation of their relationship—good friends helping each other out.

It was not too long before Kristi and David had stopped seeing other people, and they began to date. Within a year they were engaged, and eighteen months after meeting they were married. While their parents wondered if they shouldn't wait until Kristi graduated before they married, everyone agreed that Kristi and David just seemed to fit together.

After college, David felt a calling to attend seminary. Kristi shared this calling, and she planned to work to help David get through graduate school. Kristi was able to find employment in the area of management, which she truly enjoyed and where her organizational skills were valued. Within her management position, Kristi's talent for leadership and organization was quickly identified. She found herself being asked to take on large projects. This responsibility excited her and it was a boost to her self-esteem. These projects would sometimes need to be done over weekends.

David knew how much Kristi liked her job and how she wanted to do well in it, so he offered to help her on weekends. He valued Kristi's financial contribution to his education, and he also saw her confidence and self-esteem grow with each new project accomplished. In turn, Kristi understood David's passion for his vocation and realized ministry was an excellent fit for him. She wanted him to pursue his dream and was glad she had likewise found fulfillment in what she was doing.

After David graduated from seminary he began to receive calls from different churches. One snowy February day, Kristi got a call at work from David. He was breathless with excitement because he had heard from two churches that were interested in him. One church was located in Kristi's hometown. It was a small church, but had a committed congregation. The other church was larger and more prestigious with a rich history in their denomination. This larger church was three states away from where Kristi grew up.

After work, Kristi drove through the snow and congested traffic. Her heart was heavy. David worked so hard to get through seminary and now finally he would have a church of his own. But she wondered how she could consider moving three states away from her father, especially since he had recently been in declining health. Yet, she just couldn't ask David to give up this large church.

David was waiting with a celebration dinner. He had cooked a frozen pizza. Kristi forced a smile and gave him a big hug.

"Can you believe it, Kristi? Who would have thought I'd get a call from two churches!"

"I believe it, David. You've worked so hard for this. You've always wanted to be a senior minister."

As David looked out their apartment window at the busy street, he asked the question they both dreaded, "How do you feel leaving this city behind?"

Avoiding eye contact, Kristi said, "Great!"

In between bites of his pizza David spoke excitedly about his new prospects. Meanwhile Kristi half-heartedly looked through the glossy informational material from the large church.

David stopped eating and looked at Kristi. "Why are you looking at those?"

Kristi tried to brighten up and said, "Because I want to know more about my husband's new church!"

"Kristi, I know you want to be closer to your dad. I'm not taking *that* church."

Kristi reached across the table and threw her arms around David. "Oh, David, thank you. I didn't want to throw a wet blanket on your good news, but I was so worried about leaving Dad."

David kissed Kristi and then looked her in the eyes and said, "And besides, the big church wanted me to come on staff as an associate, not the senior pastor position like the smaller church."

"You stinker," she laughed, playfully pushing him away.

Twenty years later David and Kristi are still balancing. Kristi heads a division of a management company. She hosts other managers visiting from out of town, and David has learned to cook to help out at home. Kristi brings her management skills to David's parish and has assisted in getting several areas of ministry up and running. They've both been winners in their careers and in their relationship.

THE PAIN OF SELF-DISCOVERY IS
WORTH NOTHING UNLESS IN
FINDING OURSELVES WE ALSO FIND
EACH OTHER.

Cynthia J. Symonds

Who Should Control the Money?

Danielle and Peter were once again fighting over money issues. Peter had historically taken control of their finances.

Peter knew details about what they had financially and only talked vaguely when Danielle inquired about their finances. When Danielle asked for money, he would give her what she needed. But he did not like the way she recently had demanded more and more money. He sulked. She pleaded. They were in a stalemate.

Danielle was ready to begin a new job and part of the position was a more professional wardrobe. She had told Peter several times that she needed $500 to buy some new clothes. He either told her "no" or avoided the topic altogether. As the starting date of her new job grew closer Danielle grew increasingly frustrated.

"Peter, I have to get those new clothes soon because my job starts next week."

"You have plenty of good clothes to wear," Peter responded. "Besides, I don't like your attitude and we don't have the money right now!"

In a lunch conversation with a female friend, Danielle cried as she talked about the situation. Her friend assured her that Peter was being unfair, and that she should follow her conscience. Danielle got up the nerve and went shopping. After charging some new clothes without his approval, Peter went into a rage.

"What were you thinking of? How could you do such a dumb thing? You know I didn't give you permission to get those clothes! Take them back!"

Whenever they had argued in the past Danielle would complain calmly, but this time, her anger overcame her. "Peter, over the past couple of years, you've spent thousands of dollars on tools that we don't really need, and I hardly complained. You feel the freedom to spend pretty much what you please without consulting with me. You don't ask for my approval. Why should I ask you for your approval to purchase clothes I need for a new job?"

Danielle had never spoken so directly about money before. Peter was stunned. He stared silently and then stormed out of the house.

Peter went out for a long drive to cool down. He loved Danielle and didn't like to see her angry and hurt. Only money kept coming up between them. Gradually, he admitted to himself that what Danielle said was true. He spent money just as he wished. She never complained about that.

While Peter was gone, Danielle felt both anxiety and relief. She was worried about Peter's reaction to her outburst and had no idea what he would do when he returned home. On the other hand, she felt glad to have said her piece. She was proud of herself.

The hours passed and there was no Peter. When Danielle heard the door open and close, anxiety knotted her stomach. She didn't know what to expect. Peter could be mean, but he could also be so kind.

Bouquet of flowers in hand, Peter apologized. "I'm sorry for the way I have been acting. I want you to keep the clothes." He didn't say anything more, then went straight to bed.

The next day the tension had eased but still lingered in the air between them. After a few days of light conversation, Peter finally asked Danielle if they could talk about their financial situation. Danielle wondered what he had in mind. Because he had controlled this subject so much in their marriage, she couldn't help but wonder if this was another step in keeping hold of the money.

Peter disarmed her when he suggested going out to dinner. When they arrived at the restaurant, Peter handed Danielle an envelope. She opened it and as she read the handwritten note she began to cry.

> My beloved, Danielle, you have been the light of my life and a wonderful companion. In all our years together you have rarely ever complained to me about my spending. You have supported me in my hobbies, and you have always had a gracious spirit. Thank you! In the past few days I have done a lot of thinking, and we need to make some changes in how we handle money. Just like we make decisions together in so many others of our marriage we need to make decisions regarding money together as well. Please forgive me for the many times I have been insensitive to you about money. Love, Peter.

The letter and the conversation that followed opened a new chapter in their marriage. Now they both work on the family budget. They both have a fair allowance for the spending money they need. More important, by sharing the burdens of money, they bought something even more precious: peace and harmony in their relationship.

IF YOU SEEK WELLNESS BY LOVING
AND CARING FOR YOURSELF WITH
NO REGARD FOR YOUR NEIGHBOR,
YOU CANNOT BE WHOLE. IF YOU TRY
LOVING YOUR NEIGHBOR WITHOUT
ALSO LOVING AND CARING FOR
YOURSELF, GOD HELP YOUR
NEIGHBOR. NEITHER OF YOU WILL
BE WHOLE.

Nancy Loving Tubesing and
Donald A. Tubesing

WAY 9 :

Help
One Another

HOW BEAUTIFUL, HOW GRAND AND
LIBERATING THIS EXPERIENCE IS,
WHEN COUPLES LEARN . . . TO HELP
EACH OTHER.

Paul Tournier

The act of helping each other is an invaluable way to bring a greater sense of solidarity to one's marriage. Lending a helping hand to lighten the load of your spouse seems an obvious element of developing a committed relationship. But the helping needs to be a regular, conscious choice.

Alice and Cal love to surprise each other with small acts of helping. Both Alice and Cal share grocery shopping duty, though Alice will always prepare the proper coupons for her husband to take with him. For his part, Cal will often call before leaving work to see if there is anything he can pick up at the store on the way home. He tries to remember to buy the heavier items like large bottles of detergent, gallons of milk and juice, and liters of pop so that Alice does not have to carry many heavy items into the house. When either of them hears that the other has arrived home from grocery shopping, they are ready to help carry things into the house.

Cal also doesn't mind being in his car, so when their children need rides somewhere he is more apt to offer to take them and pick them up. Alice will more often work with the children on homework or fold laundry. Small acts of help not only save time and energy, but they signify care and courtesy for one another. These in themselves may be the most important reasons for consciously helping one another.

A common area of discord in marriage relationships is the fair division of household responsibilities. Today, this is a more likely problem since an increasing number of couples both work outside the home. Unless they make conscious efforts to help each other, resentments can mount and tempers flare.

Being open and willing to help needs to be an ongoing attitude because every time there is a major change within the relationship the responsibilities change. For instance, when a couple has children, they quickly realize that their established schedules and modes of working together must be adapted. Or, if one of the couple needs to spend additional hours at their job, the other may need to help out more at home. So, helping needs to be an ongoing process—readily reviewed and mutually discerned.

Zack and Denise came in for counseling because they were angry at each other about household responsibilities. Each felt like they were being taken advantage of by the other in the areas of household chores and child-care for their two young children. Before having children, Denise taught full-time. Both gladly cut back on some other leisure activities once the

children were born and they divided household chores
pretty evenly. With the birth of their second child,
Denise began to feel overwhelmed. When the three
month maternity leave ended, she went back to
teaching full-time. A child-care provider was used. Still,
each evening Denise had at least two hours of
preparation to do for the next day of class. Zack, too,
would come home tired from work. And they still had
two small children to care for in the evenings.

With these increased responsibilities, Denise had
fewer hours to keep up the house. She expected more
help from Zack. They both grew increasingly frustrated
with so much to do. The time they had to themselves as
a couple had diminished and neither of them had time
for their personal interests. They both realized that they
were going to wear out if they kept up their current
pace.

Zack worked in a business where flexible
scheduling and part-time work were not options, but
Denise was able to cut back to half-time. Within two
months they were into their new schedule and
everything was going better. Denise was enjoying her
job-sharing arrangement. She now had time to give
more attention to household needs. There was less
tension between Zack and Denise during the evenings
and weekends with this new schedule. In fact, they
both were able to fit in some leisure time to pick up old
interests.

However, matters took another turn. Without
having to help as much around the house, Zack began
spending even less time at home. He worked more and
rejoined a bowling league. Feeling cheated by Zack's
newfound freedom, Denise began going out more with
her friends during the daytime and slacked off on some
chores around the house. Then the couple started
arguing about how the house looked, who should be

taking care of the children, and the amount of time that both were using to do things other than work or care for the children.

As tensions escalated, Zack and Denise had stopped helping one another. They stopped listening and negotiating. Something had to give. During our counseling sessions, they rediscovered the sense of fulfillment they both had felt in the early days of their marriage when they spontaneously helped each other. Before children the urge to help came unconsciously. As their life became more complicated, they needed to be more conscious in their decisions to help.

At our final meeting, Zack smiled and said, "You know, I feel pretty dumb."

"How's that?" I asked.

"We've been paying you for counseling," he laughed, "when all we needed to do was ask each other how we could be of more help to each other. I mean, it isn't rocket science."

"No, it isn't rocket science. It's more complicated. You build a rocket, fire it into space, and it's more or less done. Helping each other is a lifetime task that keeps having to be built over and over."

WHAT WE CANNOT ENDURE IS THE
EXPERIENCE OF BEING UTTERLY
ALONE, WITHOUT ANYONE TO LOVE
US OR CARE ABOUT US.

David Mace

Help One Another

- Together, look at how household chores can be distributed fairly. Talk about how chores can be a way of nurturing your relationship.

- If you are caring for aging parents, children, or have other responsibilities that are taxing you, sit down together and list outside resources that could assist you. Don't be afraid to seek help.

- Surprise your partner by doing something that he or she ordinarily does in the usual division of responsibilities.

- Make a list of the types of ways that you already help each other. Make a list of the ways that you could help each other more often. Compare lists.

- Share with each other what it means to you when the other helps in some practical way.

- Sometimes we don't help with a task simply because we don't know how. You can break the chains of ignorance. Let you partner be your teacher. Pick one thing that each of you could learn from the other and then teach each other the new skill.

THE REALITY IS THAT WE DESPERATELY NEED EACH OTHER NOT MERELY FOR SUSTENANCE, NOT MERELY FOR COMPANY, BUT FOR ANY MEANING TO OUR LIVES WHATSOEVER. . . . WE CANNOT BE TRULY OURSELVES UNTIL WE ARE ABLE TO SHARE FREELY THE THINGS WE MOST HAVE IN COMMON.

M. Scott Peck

From Abuse to Affirmation

Irene showed me a faded scar on her forehead that she covered with her hair. "That scar is Christmas Eve 1976," she said. Clothing covered her other scares, and she told me that she had a date and event for each scar. She tried to explain to me why she had stayed in an abusive marriage for twenty-five years.

Her senior year of high school, she became pregnant. After graduation she married Jimmy, her high school sweetheart. It didn't seem too long after the baby was born that the abuse began. In the beginning, she explained, it was in the form of mild verbal abuse when Jimmy was irritable. Jimmy worked in his family's very successful business but hated taking orders from his father while on the job. Lots of times, he took his stresses of dealing with his father out on his wife.

Irene found that if she kept things running smoothly at home the atmosphere was less tense. Her life became a series of complex endeavors to keep Jimmy happy. After five years of marriage, they had three children and the abuse had become more severe. Jimmy both verbally and physically abused Irene, used the children against her, made threats, and played an endless string of mind games. He also controlled all of their money.

Irene felt it was a good week if only household property got broken instead of her getting hurt. At times she thought she was going crazy, and at other times she believed Jimmy when he told her that she deserved to be hit. She became adept at learning Jimmy's moods and adjusting her behavior accordingly.

To the community, Jimmy appeared to be a model citizen. Local people were grateful for the jobs Jimmy's company provided. Jimmy served on the church board and was a charitable giver to local volunteer organizations. He coached his children's teams. Irene was an avid volunteer at the schools, at church, and with civic organizations. She was a caring and loving mother and friend. To everyone, they appeared to be a committed and close couple.

Once when she had to be treated for a beating, Irene complained about her clumsiness. No one ever asked her about her bruises, and she was too scared and ashamed to tell about the abuse.

When the children were of age, they left home as soon as they could. Now alone with him, one morning Jimmy and Irene had an argument. Jimmy lashed out and gave Irene a bloody lip. He quickly left for work, taking off at break-neck speed. Irene had forgotten that she had asked her friend Julie over for coffee that morning. While she tried to put ice on her swollen bloodied lip, Julie knocked on the door. Irene at first tried to explain away her injury, but finally the whole story came tumbling out.

Julie got Irene to a doctor who, in turn, got her professional and legal help. Irene moved out of the house shortly afterwards. For his part, Jimmy refused to see that he had a problem. Finally, they divorced.

Irene was starting over at age forty-three. She moved to another part of town and got a new job. For the first year she didn't know how to cope with this new-found freedom. She wasn't sure about what type of furniture to buy for her apartment or even what to make for dinner. She had always planned everything according to Jimmy's preferences in order to keep him happy and calm.

She discovered that she enjoyed photography and, while taking a photography class, she met Ken. Ken's wife had passed away four years before. He spoke fondly of her and his marriage. Irene liked his hearty laugh and warm sense of humor. They began to date. They met each other's grown children—including Ken's mentally challenged son, Rick—and within a year they were married. This wounded woman not only loved Ken, she tenderly cared for Rick. Irene would spend hours playing cards with Rick. She always had Rick's favorite treats on-hand and introduced him to stamp collecting.

Irene was happy in her new marriage, but the legacy of her first marriage was still present. Because of the excruciating abuse she had endured, Irene now suffered constant, severe headaches. Ken was attentive to her, taking her to her doctor's appointments, picking up her medicine, and even massaging her throbbing temples in the middle of the night.

One weekend while Ken was on a fishing trip with a friend, Irene drove his new car to the supermarket. She enjoyed driving the car and could see why Ken loved it so much. While in the supermarket Irene began to experience one of her headaches. She could tell it would be extraordinarily severe. It felt like a steel band gripping her head tighter and tighter. She had no medicine in her purse to stop the pain and soon she became nauseous.

She quickly left her almost-full shopping cart in the isle and ran out of the supermarket. She barely made it to the car before she had to vomit. She got in the car and tried to drive home as best as she could, barely able to see with the blinding headache. As she turned onto a street near her home, another wave of nausea swept over her. As she hit the brakes, the car swerved on some gravel, went up on the curb, and into a neighbor's tree.

Irene's head began to bleed. She didn't notice this wound as she stumbled out of the car to see the damage. The car was wrecked. Irene sat down on the lawn and sobbed. A neighbor ran from her house to help.

That next day Irene hardly noticed her bruised and bleeding head and the excruciating headache. She sat trembling under her bedcovers, waiting to hear Ken turn the key in the front door. As she tried to sleep, she had horrible flashbacks to the years of beatings, black eyes, busted lips, broken bones, and hair torn from its roots. Her body remembered, and she ached from head to toe. She heard the front door open quickly and slam. She knew Ken must have seen his wrecked car in the driveway. She heard his heavy footsteps on the stairs as he raced to the bedroom. She leapt from the bed and crouched in the corner.

She screamed, "No, no, no, please, please don't hurt me."

Ken rushed to her, "Irene, are you alright? My God, when I saw the car I thought you were dead. Please, honey, tell me you're okay."

Sobbing, she fell into his arms. "I'm sorry, Ken. I'm so sorry."

"It's okay, Irene. We'll get it fixed."

"Yes, but, Ken, I'm sorry for thinking you would hurt me."

Ken rocked her in his arms, drying her tears, and soothing her. All that went through his mind was gratitude that he had found love again. The years of abuse had not taken away her gentle spirit.

Even as he held her like this—sobbing and scared— Ken loved her even more.

When her tears subsided, Ken helped her back to bed. "Rest, Irene. You've had a terrible ordeal. I'm so glad you're not hurt. I'm so glad you're my wife. Can I get you anything before I go?"

"No, dear Ken. Just please forgive me for doubting you."

"Honey, it's already done. Now get some rest."

Irene cried quietly again, but this time tears of gratitude and joy.

TWO PEOPLE CAN ACCOMPLISH MORE THAN TWICE AS MUCH AS ONE; THEY GET A BETTER RETURN FOR THEIR LABOR. IF ONE PERSON FALLS, THE OTHER CAN REACH OUT AND HELP. BUT PEOPLE WHO ARE ALONE WHEN THEY FALL ARE IN REAL TROUBLE.

Ecclesiastes

I Want To Help You

Although middle-aged, Pat and Lorraine have only been married one year. Pat's wife died eight years ago and Lorraine has been divorced for ten years.

They knew each other years ago when they went to the same high school. Although they passed each other every day at school, they moved in different social circles and didn't get to know each other very well. Pat was the all-star football player and hung out with the sport's crowd. Lorraine played in the orchestra and hung out with other musicians. Lorraine and Pat became reacquainted when they returned for their thirty-fifth high school reunion.

Pat was now a successful building contractor, and Lorraine was a high school music teacher. Pat enjoyed Lorraine's easy manner with people, and Lorraine appreciated Pat's quick wit and self confidence. Their courtship was brief and they married just six months after the reunion.

They decided to sell their respective homes and purchase a condominium. When they were signing the purchase agreement right before they married, Lorraine noticed that Pat was squinting. During the few months that they were dating there were several times that Lorraine noticed that Pat was having trouble with his eyes.

Lorraine urged Pat to see an eye doctor. She thought he was just being stubborn with advancing age and not giving into the fact that his eyesight had changed. She saw how it affected his work because his secretary had to read his letters to him. One night when his grandson wanted Pat to read a story to him, Pat offered to tell an imaginary story because "Grandpa's eyes are tired."

For several months, Lorraine urged Pat to get his eyes checked. He kept delaying. So one Saturday morning Lorraine offered to drive Pat to their usual breakfast place. Instead she drove him to the eye-care center. When she pulled into the medical center Pat became angry. He refused to get out of the car. Lorraine was incredulous that he put up such a protest and was really confused as to why he flatly refused to take care of his own health. Pat got into the driver's seat and drove them home.

Lorraine couldn't stand the tension in the house that day, so she left to have dinner with a friend. She took the long way home that night, thinking things over as she drove. She puzzled over Pat's peculiar behavior concerning his eyes.

It was late when she got to their condo, and she quietly tried to steal in so as not to disturb Pat. Once indoors she heard his voice from the den. He was speaking in a low voice, so she listened for a while. He was sounding out a familiar nursery rhyme from his grandson's book. Lorraine saw no sign of his grandson so she listened on. As she listened, Pat's "eye problem" became clear.

As she entered the den, Pat quickly put down the book. He was glad to see her, and came over to ask her forgiveness for his behavior earlier that day.

Lorraine quickly forgave him and embraced him. While she held Pat, she whispered, "Pat, why didn't you tell me?"

Pat released her, turned, and walked to the window. He couldn't look at her. Pausing, he finally said, "Because, Lorraine, I thought you would think less of me. I've told no one about this. When I was younger I was afraid I'd be teased. Now that I'm older I thought I would lose people's respect. Being on the football team in high school, they just kept passing me through the grades. It didn't matter to them that I didn't know how to read. Scoring a touchdown was all that mattered then."

Lorraine took Pat's clenched fists into her hands. "It matters to me, Pat. Not for my sake, but for yours."

"Well, it's too late now, Lorraine, I've gotten by on my wits until now and I guess I'll just keep on doing so."

Lorraine lifted his chin. "Pat, you're right. Your wits have gotten you this far and your wits will help you learn how to read. And I want to help you. Let me help you."

"How can you respect a grown man who can't read?"

"Pat, I love you and I respect you. Please let me help."

Pat walked back to the coffee table, gazed at the nursery book, and picked it up. He sat down on the couch again. After what seemed like a long time to Lorraine, he opened the first page. Lorraine sat down beside him as he began to sound out the first sentence.

TO MARRY IS TO GET A BINOCULAR VIEW OF LIFE.

William Inge

WAY 10:

Resolve Conflicts Before They Get Worse

THE CONCEPTION OF TWO PEOPLE
LIVING TOGETHER FOR TWENTY-FIVE
YEARS WITHOUT HAVING A CROSS
WORD SUGGESTS A LACK OF SPIRIT
ONLY TO BE ADMIRED IN SHEEP.

Alan Patrick Herbert

Maureen enjoys the opening ten minutes of
television news so, during that time, she likes me
to be quiet. Since I have less interest in those ten
minutes, I tend to chat with her. She gets frustrated
with me. Twenty minutes later the roles reverse. When
I want to watch the sports, she tries to chat with me. We
both talk during the weather.

Conflict in a marital relationship is normal, but it
has daily implications. Disagreements can flare up
about how warm or cool to keep the home or whether
to have one or two blankets on the bed. When a couple
marries, there are now two voices, two opinions, and
two votes to be heard on many decisions. Dealing with

and resolving our inevitable conflicts can become defining moments in any marriage.

Probably the greatest area of conflict that two of our clients—Judy and Sam—have had through the years is over parenting their children. They both agree that all children need structure, challenge, and discipline as well as comfort, love, and mercy. However, how these values get carried out in practical ways is another story.

Sam leans on the side of tolerance and mercy. He grew up in a tolerant home and never remembers a single spanking. While also a loving person, Judy grew up in a more disciplined family than Sam's. She remembers spankings and stiff penalties. So when major conflicts occur about their children, Sam emphasizes flexibility and forgiveness, while Judy encourages boundaries and consequences. Either Judy or Sam could just back down when they engage in arguments over raising their kids. That might seem to work occasionally and in the short run, but usually the one acquiescing the most ends up carrying a load of resentment. Or, they might avoid resolving the conflict, then they *both* carry resentment. Either way, tensions would most likely just fester and eventually poison the relationship.

For a successful marriage, partners need to accept that disagreements are normal, to not be scared of conflict, and to see conflict as an opportunity for communication and intimacy. Then they need to keep in mind some keen advice from Don Dinkmeyer and Jon Carlson who suggest these two steps in dealing with conflict in marriage:

> *Step 1. Show Mutual Respect.* Rather than the issue itself, the attitude of one or both partners is often at the heart of the conflict. In a relationship with mutual respect, each partner seeks to understand and respect the other's point of view.

Step 2. Pinpoint the Real Issue. Most couples have difficulty identifying the real issue. Who does what around the house, how money is spent, or whether or not to have sex usually are not the real issues. These disagreements do have to be resolved, of course. But the purpose or goal the partner is trying to achieve is the real issue. Once the real issue is identified it becomes easier to resolve surface disagreements.

Without mutual respect and a sense of what is really at issue, conflicts tend to go round in circles. David and Vera Mace outline three ways to break a tie when we are struggling to resolve our differences:

1. Capitulation means that one partner freely gives in to go in the direction of the other. For this approach to work, both parties each need to capitulate an equal number times. If one capitulates ninety-five times while the other does so only five times, capitulation ceases to be effective and honest.

2. Compromise means each partner gives some ground in order to come to a decision. In the case of a curfew for a child: one parent might want a midnight deadline and the other 1:00 a.m., so they split the difference and agree on 12:30 a.m.

3. Co-existence means each party agreeing to disagree and operating differently on the matter. Of course, in some matters, co-existence just won't work well. Some decisions have to be made whether both partners can agree or not.

On many decisions facing a couple, any of these three approaches could be used.

If two people respect each other and honestly work out the truth of a matter, capitulation robs neither person of dignity. Coming to compromise may actually be a good time to learn more about each other. Co-existence—taking different directions over an issue—can be healthy. The only thing more troublesome than resolving conflicts is not resolving them.

> A POWER STRUGGLE CAN BE ENDED
> ONLY WHEN ALL PARTIES AGREE TO
> FULL RESPONSIBILITY FOR THE
> CREATION OF THE ISSUE.
>
> *Kathlyn and Gay Hendricks*

Resolve Conflicts Before They Get Worse

- Identify and name the types of things that bring tension and conflict in your relationship.

- What do you do as a couple to solve your conflicts? How well do your strategies work? What are some changes that you need to make to handle conflict?

- Own your feelings. Avoid blaming. To follow this approach use "I messages" (e.g., "I am really angry!") messages instead of "you messages" (e.g., "You really make me angry!"). Think about a recent disagreement you had with your partner. Try to formulate "I messages" that express your truth but do not accuse, blame, or project onto your partner. Say these "I messages" out loud and note how they feel. Next time you get into a disagreement, try "I messages." They just might help.

- Practice using "capitulation, compromise, and co-existence" in settling a variety of situations in which there is no agreement. It can help when both you and your spouse determine the approach to take.

- Think back on some of the disagreements and arguments you have had with each other. Who usually "wins" the arguments? How do you respond when your partner wins an argument? How do you respond when you win an argument? What does this response say about your relationship?

- Consider this statement from the Bible about resolving conflicts. Talk about how it might apply to your partnership: "Let everything you say be good and helpful, so that your words will be an encouragement to those who hear them . . . Get rid of all bitterness, rage, anger, harsh words, and slander, as well as all types of malicious behavior" (Ephesians 4:29-30).

IN ITSELF, QUARRELLING CAN BE QUITE HELPFUL IF IT REVEALS THE DEEPER FEELINGS OF HUSBAND AND WIFE TO EACH OTHER. . . . AS LONG AS COUPLES KNOW JUST WHY THEY QUARRELED, THEY CAN AND SHOULD MAKE THE NECESSARY ADJUSTMENTS SO THAT THEY NEEDN'T REPEAT THAT QUARREL.

David Mace

Please Stay

In Dublin, Ireland in 1910, only the fittest survived. My father would tell us stories of harsh living in the inner city of Dublin where rampant unemployment and poverty was equally matched with illness and death.

Aggie and Patrick lived on the top floor of a tenement house in the heart of the city. Aggie had hair as black as night, and it reached down to her waist. Her eyes were just as dark and were fiery to match her spirit. She was a liberated woman before her time who championed women's causes.

She was the unofficial social worker in her community. Aggie was often called on to assist other women who were in labor and giving birth. She visited the sick, she washed the dying and the dead, and she gave what she could to those less fortunate than herself. She had great compassion for the women who lived in poverty, whose children suffered with hunger and devastating childhood illness. She and Patrick and their own family lived alongside others in the chilly, damp, packed rooms without adequate facilities—where children were lucky to reach the age of five.

Patrick was a whiskey blender for a large brewery in the center of the city. He was a hard worker, a friendly man, a loving husband and father. Patrick and Aggie grew up together on the same street. Their families shared with each other when food was scarce. Patrick was good at his job and over time he developed a liking for his craft and its product. His dependence on alcohol was slow and insidious, yet Aggie was beginning to see changes in his attitude and his behavior.

While Aggie cared for others in her close-knit community, she had her own share of troubles. By the time she was thirty, she had seven children. The threat of tuberculosis hung over the community, and people were hyper-vigilant of any sign of an outbreak. The time came when Aggie's own children contracted the dreaded disease, and she helplessly watched them slip away one after another. Her home had been a household of noise and laughter. But by the time the epidemic had burned itself out, her brood of children was devastated. She was left with only two children, whom she guarded with her life.

Soon after the outbreak of tuberculoses the economy turned even more foul, poverty and disease increased, and unemployment became the norm. Patrick's brewery went out of business, and he had no job. Aggie and Patrick lost their home. During these troubled times he sought comfort and solace with the other unemployed men at the local pub. Usually by the time he left the pub the day was gone and so was the money. This went on for several months. Aggie pleaded, cried, got angry, and threatened, but all this emotion fell on Patrick's deaf ears.

One cold, wet, night Patrick stumbled his way home as usual from the pub. Falling down in the slippery lane he picked himself up with his wet muddy clothes sticking to his shivering body. He struggled his way up the stairs in the tenement until he reached the top floor where he and Aggie lived. He pounded on the door. It limply swung open. Inside the room it was dark and silent. He stood swaying before the cold fireplace, taking in the scene. When his eyes adjusted to the darkness he saw a note propped up against the mantle piece. He lit a candle on the kitchen table and sat down.

As his eyes adjusted he began to read it. His lips moved rapidly as he read and then reread the note. At that point he jumped up from the table, ran to the bedroom, and without a light could see the empty beds. He raced from the apartment and stumbled down the stairs into the foggy night, scrambling through the city streets like a man running from death. He heard the ships' horns blow before he got to the docks. He hoped he could get to Aggie in time because if she got on that boat he might never see her or their two little boys again.

When he turned the corner that led to the docks his eyes widened at the sight of the throng of people sitting and standing in the rain ready to board the ship. Lines had formed as people with their bundles struggled up the gangplank. Patrick frantically searched through the crowds for Aggie, but the huddled souls under the beating rain all looked the same to him. Suddenly he saw the familiar red shawl. He spun her around.

Her eyes flew open when she saw Patrick, standing drenched and shivering. The two little boys each grabbed his legs and clung to their father. Patrick pleaded with Aggie to stay.

He couldn't interpret her expression as she gazed up at the ship that was shrouded in the fog. Her face softened as she set down her battered suitcase. Patrick grabbed her, holding her so tight, all the while realizing how close he had come to losing his family.

They made their way back through the narrow lanes and streets. Aggie carried the suitcase. Patrick carried a sleeping boy in each arm. Once into their rooms, Aggie put the boys to bed while Patrick lit a fire. Aggie still hadn't said much, and Patrick knew he was the one who had to speak first.

Patrick cleared his throat. "Aggie, I know how terrible this has been for you—the loss of my job and all, my drinking away what little money we had left. I just got so down, Aggie—a man has his pride ya' know."

Aggie turned her head away and Patrick caught himself. "I know, I know, Aggie. I shouldn't be giving you excuses. I'm sorry."

They sat in silence for a while. "Aggie, we both have suffered, and I realize I left you taking care of our troubles while I found comfort in a whiskey bottle. I was no comfort to you. I just added to your misery and for that I'm very, very sorry. I ask for your forgiveness. I know that it will take a lot of work on my part to earn your trust back. Losing you tonight nearly killed me."

Aggie stood up and blew out the candle. He clung to her, and she stroked his wet hair. She wanted to talk to him, to reassure him, but she just couldn't speak. She was just too worn down with the constant struggle to survive and, just as the sun was rising, she went to bed for a short rest.

That morning while Aggie was hanging their wet clothes out to dry, Patrick appeared in the garden and behind him was Father Matthews, a kind and friendly old parish priest. He had not only married Aggie and Patrick, but he had baptized them as infants and officiated at the burials of their children. Aggie brought Father Matthews up to their rooms for some tea.

While Patrick made the tea, Father Matthews explained that Patrick came to his church early that morning to talk to the priest about his drinking, unemployment, and the troubles he and Aggie had endured. Father Matthews had agreed to help Patrick. Patrick agreed to meet weekly with the parish priest to talk about his problems with alcohol. He had agreed to stop drinking, and Father Matthews gave him the name of a friend who had a bicycle repair shop who was looking for an assistant. Patrick planned to meet very soon with the repair shop owner.

When Father Matthews stopped talking, Aggie started to smile. "Thank you, Father. The troubles just got too big for both of us. I just couldn't go on the way it was. I pray we can go on now."

Hearing this, Patrick murmured Aggie's last words in his own prayer, and prayed that he would never let matters between them go so badly again.

Anger is meant to be acted upon. It is not meant to be acted out.

Julia Cameron

For Sale

Lisa and Perry Albright met while working for the same company. Perry was attracted to Lisa's natural enthusiasm and her warmth towards people. It was no wonder she was one of the top sales producers in the company. Lisa appreciated Perry's drive, his managerial style, and his ability to rally his team to meet deadlines. Just when their relationship became serious, Lisa took a job with another company. Both believed this move was good for their relationship since too much time together was spent in shoptalk. Perry's co-workers were not surprised when Perry announced his and Lisa's engagement. A wedding was planned shortly thereafter.

Three years later the neighbors watched as the "For Sale" sign was placed in the Albright's yard. Perry was the first one home that evening and saw the "For Sale" sign. He sat for a while in the driveway, looking at the sign. A faint smile crossed his lips before he grabbed his briefcase and headed through the front door. Lisa was home a half-hour later with Cody and Cassy, their two-year-old twins.

Perry was already halfway through fixing dinner and the smell of food cooking was much appreciated by Lisa. This serene family scene was not how it used to be for the Albright family. Less than a year ago the family dinner hour would be filled with screaming adults and crying babies. Perry would grab his food and take off towards the television in the bedroom, or sometimes Lisa would lock herself in the bathroom and wouldn't emerge for almost an hour. In fact, the Albrights' home was so large, Perry and Lisa had many rooms from which to choose to avoid each other.

Lisa and Perry had found this dream house just three years ago. With their combined incomes they thought they could afford it although they knew it would be really tight. That was before Lisa got pregnant with the twins, Perry's company laid off some employees, and he had to take a pay cut. With these changes the Albrights decided they'd just have to work harder and tighten their belts. This worked for a while, but physical exhaustion, tension, and anxiety set in.

Perry became despondent and had difficulty going to work every day. Some days he called in sick, took the twins to daycare, and went back home and played on the computer. Lisa became infuriated. She'd nag at Perry, but even while he would make promises not to do this again, he knew that he'd break those promises. Then Lisa decided to get even.

Shopping became a tension release for her and soon the bills piled up, unopened in their newly furnished home office. Lisa also charged some new outfits even though she had several dresses with tags still on hangers in her walk-in closet. And even in the midst of their growing financial problems, Perry and Lisa borrowed some money and made a trip to a nearby riverboat casino.

With cash now a major problem, they both began asking their parents and relatives for loans. Soon their support network began to dwindle. Perry finally realized how serious a problem they had. The runaway train of self-destruction finally came to a halt when their daycare provider put the Albrights on notice because two of their checks had bounced. That night after the twins were put to bed, Lisa and Perry sat in their office, finally sorting through the bills. The anger had fizzled to an overwhelming sense of despair. They knew they were in trouble and needed help fast.

Perry looked at Lisa and asked, "How did this happen to us?"

Lisa sat, head bent. She answered by shaking her head. "How could we be so dumb?" Tears were welling up in her eyes, blinding her as she looked at the bank statements and the amounts of money they owed. Perry came and sat beside her. They both felt heartsick and scared.

"What is wrong with us, Lisa?" He stood, started to pace the floor, and began listing how much they owed and to whom. His anger and frustration began to build. Lisa listened to Perry, and her anger also began to grow. Soon they were blaming each other and yelling until the twins woke up with the noise and began to cry.

After the twins were finally asleep again, Lisa and Perry were both too exhausted to argue. "This isn't helping, Lisa." Perry put his arm around her. "We can't keep blaming each other, but we do have to figure out how to get out of the mess we created." That evening they sat down together, each with a calculator and notepaper, and began to look for ways to reach their common goal: getting out of debt.

The next day Perry made an appointment for them to meet with their bank manager. After several meetings with the bank and a financial counselor, they decided to sell the house and pay off their debts. Lisa had found a nice home, though much smaller.

After the movers had pulled away from the curb, Lisa and Perry watched as the twins played amidst the boxes.

"We've got a new start, Lisa. Let's do it better this time."

"Yes, better and together."

TO KEEP YOUR MARRIAGE BRIMMING, WITH LOVE IN THE WEDDING CUP, WHENEVER YOU'RE WRONG, ADMIT IT; WHENEVER YOU'RE RIGHT, SHUT UP.

Ogden Nash

Readily Forgive and Reconcile If Possible

WE CANNOT LOVE UNLESS WE HAVE
ACCEPTED FORGIVENESS, AND THE
DEEPER   OUR   EXPERIENCE   OF
FORGIVENESS IS, THE GREATER OUR
LOVE.

Paul Tillich

Forgiving and giving up resentment are two great
challenges in marriage—actually in any relationship.
In a relationship that lacks forgiveness, alienation creeps
into the marriage like an unwelcome guest who
constantly meddles and spreads seeds of doubt in each
partner's ear. However, forgiveness is not something
that happens instantaneously and spontaneously. Most
of us need to do it consciously and carefully. But if our
marriage is to thrive, do it we must.

One weekend Julie packed her bags and left her
husband, Tim. For years Tim had heaped verbal abuse
on Julie. She would cry and then become distant. He
would apologize. She would forgive him, and then he

would verbally abuse her again. The cycle continued over and over. Finally, she had enough.

When I saw Julie, she was filled with anger, hurt, and guilt. She was angry and hurt because of the abuse. She felt guilty because she thought that she should always forgive Tim and perhaps should not have walked out. Clearly, Julie had a lot to sort out.

First, I needed to help Julie understand what forgiveness really is and what it is not. Forgiveness is *not* forgetting Tim's abuse or excusing it. Abuse is wrong. No one has a right to abuse another person. Julie had every right to blame Tim for his abuse. Forgiveness also is not letting people off the hook or assuming responsibility for what they did.

Robert Enright, founder of the International Forgiveness Institute at the University of Wisconsin, describes forgiveness as "giving up the resentment to which you are entitled and offering to the person who hurt you friendlier attitudes to which they are not entitled." Adds Sister Helen Prejean, author of *Dead Man Walking* and central character in the movie by the same name, "I don't see forgiveness as condoning the terrible wrong done to someone, but I see it as strength to love and not letting hate and bitterness take over my life."

For Julie, then, forgiving Tim didn't mean that she should permit the abuse or that she should condone Tim's actions. Forgiving meant that she could—in her own time—give up her resentment to which she was entitled and still have a positive, even loving attitude, towards Tim. Equally important, by forgiving she wouldn't let hate and bitterness take over her life.

Forgiving may or may not help patch up a damaged relationship, but it is essential for our own healing. Unless Tim actually stopped his abusive behavior, reconciliation with him would probably be ill-advised.

However, forgiving Tim would empower Julie and help her move on. Forgiveness is a decision we make, unconnected to the worthiness of the other person, and to whether they are repentant. We forgive so that *we* can let go of the bitterness and the hatred that rankle our soul—eventually destroying these negative feelings.

Some other steps move us further towards forgiveness. One positive decision is to face the full range of our feelings: our anger and hurt, our guilt and shame. And we should honestly inventory all our gifts and blessings. In other words, we take responsibility for our feelings, failings, and our power. In a sense, we are "getting ourselves together" by looking honestly at our lives.

Next, if circumstances permit, involving ourselves in a life-giving activity also helps. We do so, not to avoid the hurt, but to detach ourselves from the issue and recapture our sense of aliveness and power. So, we take a walk in a state park, play fetch with the dog, weed the garden, finish a book, or repair a favorite chair. Detaching from emotions for a while helps in serious situations like Julie's or even in minor scrapes like one partner forgetting (for the fifth time) to fill the car with gas.

Another part of the forgiveness process is to refrain from striking back or punishing. Payback ultimately just makes matters worse. Taking the almost-empty car out to run the tank down to fumes just before our spouse has to go somewhere only heightens the tensions and raw feelings. A good action would be to say nothing. A better thing would be to do some small act of kindness for our partner.

When we are ready, we consciously forgive. We can say the words out loud, at least to ourselves. We should not feel compelled to offer words of forgiveness to the other person. If the one who always leaves the tank almost empty apologizes, speak your forgiveness happily. Julie, on the other hand, can still forgive Tim, but telling him may only perpetuate the cycle of his abuse. When and if reconciliation becomes possible, she might then express her forgiveness.

Forgiveness is something you can do yourself; reconciliation requires commitment from both partners. Julie can forgive Tim, but to be reconciled to a mutually loving relationship, Tim has to make some decisions, too. He must cease the abuse. As Louis Smedes says in his book *The Art of Forgiving*: "Forgiveness has no strings attached. Reunion has several strings attached."

Most friction in marriage can be resolved through forgiveness. We all have to just let some annoyances go with a shake of the head and murmured words of forgiveness, chalking them up to our partner's idiosyncrasies. Major wrongs like Tim's abuse of Julie require much more careful consideration.

If Julie and Tim are to be reconciled, she has to ask some hard questions: How do I really feel about Tim? If we can be reconciled, what do I need to have happen and what do I want from our relationship? What's my bottom line? What will I need to say to Tim? Do I still harbor anger and resentment? (If she hasn't let go of a lot of anger and resentment, she will need to take some more time before making the next choice.)

Once Julie has the answers she needs to those questions, then she might decide to contact Tim to see how he feels about the situation. If he seems open to rebuilding the relationship, Julie might want to meet with him in a safe place and tell him what she has to tell him. If Tim seems receptive, they need to talk about what caused the problems in the first place. What is the verbal abuse about? From where is the abuse coming?

What can he do about it? And so on. For something this serious, counseling is a good idea.

Finally, Julie must then discuss what she needs and set the bottom line if they are to reconcile. Tim needs to offer more than words; he has to take hard steps to restore the relationship.

Marriage survives with forgiveness. It is a great gift we offer one another. To contradict the famous line from a movie, love means that we *often* say we're sorry. When a relationship comes apart, we still need forgiveness and hope for reconciliation.

FORGIVENESS IS NOT SOMETHING YOU DO FOR SOMEONE ELSE; IT IS SOMETHING YOU DO FOR YOURSELF. GIVE YOURSELF THE GIFT OF FORGIVENESS.

David Schell

Readily Forgive and Reconcile If Possible

- Write some of the kinds of things for which you can apologize to your spouse. Choose a recent wrong and apologize with gentle words and some simple act.

- Have you collected any resentment towards your spouse? If so, in what ways? What happened? Consider sharing this with your partner when appropriate. Remember, use "I" messages.

- Usually one thing that helps when forgiving another is to remember ways that you have been forgiven by others. Reflect on moments when you were forgiven. How did you feel? Now, to whom do you want to offer forgiveness?

* If you and your spouse need to reconcile, ask yourself the hard question posed in the introduction to this chapter: What do you need if you have been wronged? What do you need to do to rebuild the relationship if you were wrong?

THE STUPID NEITHER FORGIVE NOR FORGET; THE NAIVE FORGIVE AND FORGET; THE WISE FORGIVE BUT DO NOT FORGET.

Thomas Szasz

Drained

Beverly and Jack looked older than they really are. As they spoke about their marriage they both slumped in their chairs, not giving eye contact to the other. This was a second marriage for Beverly and a third marriage for Jack. They met at a medical clinic where Beverly worked and Jack went to get his allergy shots.

Jack has no children. Beverly has two sons. Beverly's first marriage was extremely abusive. The boys saw Beverly being beaten. She finally left when her husband began to beat the boys. Her oldest son, Ben, now 16, has always had a bad temper like his father. Both Beverly and Jack have become increasingly concerned about Ben's rages, and recently he has physically intimidated Beverly when Jack was not at home. Beverly blames herself for Ben's problem behavior. She believes she should have left her first marriage earlier because of what her two sons witnessed. Ben experienced so much violence.

Jack wants Ben to take responsibility for his actions, and urged Beverly to follow through on consequences with Ben. Beverly and Jack had been getting calls from the school for over a year now regarding her son's increasing negative behavior. He also was suspended for three days for fighting and was put on probation with the juvenile justice system for another assault. If he breaks his probation, he will be placed in juvenile detention. This is Beverly's worse nightmare. She believes that once Ben ends up in detention, he will end up a criminal just like his father.

Ben's behavior placed a terrible strain on their marriage. Jack was an ex-marine who took a no-nonsense approach to Ben. Beverly remembered the harsh treatment Ben's father dished out to him. She tried to coddle him in order to make up for his terrifying childhood.

Beverly and Jack carried on the best they could with Ben. Meanwhile Ben's brother, Jay, watched the turmoil Ben caused the family. He tried just as hard to please as Ben did to displease. One day Jack was getting ready for work. When he pulled out his wallet to give Jay some lunch money, he discovered that the $200 that he got out of the cash machine the night before was gone. He questioned Beverly, and she had not seen it. Ben had already left for school so they couldn't question him.

That night, when Jack asked Ben about the missing money, the boy flew into a rage. He then bolted out of the house.

Beverly urged Jack to wait just a few days before jumping to conclusions. A day later Jack found $200 on the floor at the foot of their bed. The $200 was in four $50 bills—not the ten $20 bills that he had gotten out of the cash machine.

At the end of the month when Jack balanced the checkbook, he noticed a withdrawal for $200 the day after he had withdrawn the original $200 from the cash machine. He didn't say anything to Beverly, but eventually it began to eat away at him.

He finally asked Beverly about the $200, and she started to cry. Apparently, Beverly had seen Ben come home with some merchandise the day after the money disappeared. She confronted Ben. While he didn't admit the theft of the $200, he couldn't give an explanation for his sudden financial windfall. The merchandise he had purchased was already opened and used. She called the store, but they would not accept anything back. Beverly knew this theft meant Ben could get into legal trouble with the juvenile authorities. She just couldn't bring herself to report the theft, so she withdrew the $200 and put it in a place where Jack would find it.

Jack was furious that Beverly lied to him and that once again she sought to protect Ben. Beverly angrily accused Jack of not understanding her or Ben and the trauma they had endured for so many years.

Jack felt defeated. There seemed no way he could compete with this powerful mother-son bond. He went ahead and called the police anyway. Ben was arrested, eventually convicted, and sentenced to some time in a juvenile facility. For a long time Beverly couldn't forgive Jack.

Now, without Ben to bring emotions to a boil, Jack and Beverly talk about many things, are learning about each other, and offering the forgiveness that heals.

ONCE A WOMAN HAS FORGIVEN
HER MAN, SHE MUST NOT REHEAT
HIS SINS FOR BREAKFAST.

Marlene Dietrich

Replaced

Wendy and Mike were the type who'd finish each other's sentences. They'd laugh at the same things and, although they had been married for ten years, they still cuddled on the couch while watching a movie. Wendy enjoyed her job as a dental hygienist and Mike worked in a men's clothing store. Their income was modest but sufficient for their needs, although Mike could occasionally get carried away buying fishing gear in a sporting goods store. Wendy was the practical one and tried to understand Mike's need to go fishing with the guys.

Their life was fairly predictable up until one year ago when Chad, one of Mike's buddies from childhood, had to move out of a house he was leasing. Chad approached Mike about the possibility of renting out their basement until he could find something else. Mike and Wendy agreed it would be okay. They had just purchased a new car and the extra income would help with their car payments. Chad moved in and the adjustment went smoothly for Mike and Wendy.

Awhile after Chad moved in, Mike's store lost a couple of employees and his boss asked him to fill in an extra weekday night and on Saturdays. While Mike didn't like the idea, Wendy and he agreed that the extra money would come in handy during the holidays.

With Mike working long hours and not getting home until much later at night, Wendy was feeling lonely and irritable. With just one television in the house, Chad would sit down with Wendy at night as they enjoyed watching the same television shows. Wendy found Chad to be funny and a good conversationalist. On nights she had to go pick up Mike from work, Chad would offer to go get him. On Sundays when they watched sports Chad joined them. Soon he was invited to several outings as if he were a new member of the family. All three joined a bowling league together.

Mike and Wendy spent less and less time as a couple. "Wendy and Mike" were really now "Wendy, Mike, and Chad"—a close threesome. And when Mike was asked to work extra hours, Chad would accompany Wendy in Mike's place to a social event or just go out with her.

After some months Mike began to take notice of Wendy and Chad's close relationship. They occasionally went out and failed to invite Mike along. Mike tried not to give it much thought, and even chided himself for having a suspicious mind.

One night when he got home late from work, Wendy and Chad were still out. He made himself some dinner and went to light up a cigarette afterwards. His lighter broke so he started to look for matches. Wendy smoked too, so he looked through her desk drawer for matches. He found a book of matches, but he also found a card to Wendy from Chad.

The card read, "To my lover." Matt was stunned. He read the card over and over in disbelief. Later that night when Wendy and Chad fell in the front door laughing together, Matt greeted them, holding the card in their faces. Furiously, he lunged for Chad. A fight ensued and Wendy had to call the police.

Mike spent the night in jail. The next day he went home for some clothes. Chad had already moved out. Wendy sat in the kitchen as Mike packed his bags. As he passed through the kitchen on his way out Wendy stepped in front of him.

"Please, Mike, don't go. I know I made a huge, horrible mistake. Please forgive me. Let's try to work this out." She pleaded as she placed a hand on his arm.

He looked at her, and she never looked more beautiful to him. But something had died in him. He felt utterly betrayed by the only woman he had ever loved and by his best friend. He took her hand and looked at it for a long moment and then without saying a word, he brushed past her, closing the door behind him.

EVERYONE SAYS FORGIVENESS IS A LOVELY IDEA UNTIL THEY HAVE SOMETHING TO FORGIVE.

C. S. Lewis

WAY 12:

Share Each Other's Joys and Sorrows

WHAT DO WOMEN MOST WANT FROM
THEIR HUSBANDS? IT IS NOT A BIGGER
HOME OR A BETTER DISHWASHER OR
A NEWER AUTOMOBILE. RATHER, IT IS
THE ASSURANCE THAT "HAND IN
HAND" WE'LL FACE THE BEST AND
WORST THAT LIFE HAS TO OFFER—
TOGETHER.

James Dobson

O n our wedding day, Maureen and I made the
following promises to each other:

I take you to be my wedded husband/wife,

I promise to love you, to be patient, kind, and
gentle;

I promise to cherish you, to honor you and be
faithful to you in all things, to give my whole
self to you.

149

I promise to sustain you in sickness as in
health,

in poverty as in wealth, in times of joy and in
times of sadness.

I promise to comfort and encourage you.

In preparation for our wedding we looked at a
number of traditional vows and put these words
together as a reflection of our desire to share our lives
together. As we made these promises to each other over
twenty years ago, we did not know what awaited us in
the years ahead. Early in marriage there was the
enjoyment of visiting a favorite restaurant near our
cozy little apartment in Rochester, New York. There
was also the common mission of working together in a
group home for difficult adolescent girls.

After moving to Duluth, Minnesota, we loved the
walks along Lake Superior one block from our home.
One morning, we shared the sadness of finding our
basement flooded when a water pipe broke. Together
we had the joy of seeing four healthy children grow up
and the consuming sadness when another child died.

We worked together as parents to care for our
family. There were the usual trips to the emergency
room with children for various injuries, and times
when our children were sick and needed special care.
We grieved together when our fourteen-year-old dog
Sammy died. There were the ongoing tasks of cleaning
the home, preparing meals, caring for children,
working jobs, and paying bills. There were leaves to
rake, lawns to cut, snow to shovel, windows to replace,
and cars to fix.

Most married couples remember times when they
were loving, patient, kind, and gentle with each other
and other times when they were unloving, impatient,
unkind, and coarse. Memories can be a blessing or a
curse, depending on how the marriage has gone.

After thirty-five years marriage Kevin and Denise had many memories of deep bonding, but also some recent years of disconnection. Now in their early sixties, Kevin had recently told Denise that he was thinking of leaving her. In the past five years, he had several things go wrong in his life and had slipped into depression. His physical health had been deteriorating and with the prescription medicine he was on, he was struggling with periodic impotence. He had missed out on a promotion at the company where he had worked for fifteen years, being bypassed by a younger man. His old cheerful self seemed to have vanished and been replaced by a bitter, frustrated, angry man. The close relationship he had always had with Denise seemed to be slipping away.

They had shared so many experiences in their years together that Kevin felt a strong pull to stay together—for himself, for Denise, and for their three grown children and grandchildren. Kevin wanted to be responsible. He always had been. Besides, he valued marriage as a lifetime proposition. But his life just seemed spiraling down hill.

Denise knew that there had been an emptiness in their relationship for a long time, but having shared in so many things together she was shocked to hear Kevin talk of separation and divorce. Denise was happy in her teaching position and was nearing retirement. They had developed their separate good friendships and hobbies, but also had some couples with whom they would get together from time to time. Everyone that knew them thought they were happy.

When they came in for counseling, Kevin shared that he felt closely connected to his three grown children and their families. For years the entire clan would gather at the family cabin on summer weekends and at the old family home periodically during the rest of the year. When Denise told their grown children that

Kevin was thinking about a divorce, they were deeply hurt and angered. The sons were confused and furious, the daughter went into depression.

Even in the midst of their turmoil and pain, Kevin and Denise acknowledged their bonds. They shared too much history, too many memories, especially within their extended family. Even though they felt emotional distance, they had slept together for thirty-five years, eaten together most evenings, shared a home and a cabin, and had countless experiences together. Together they had raised a family and now enjoyed their grandchildren. So what would they do?

The start of their reunion came as Kevin began talking about his depression, the sense of loss that came with just being older, the feeling of being shunted aside at his job, and his frustration and fear because of the impotence. Even though Denise had listened attentively before, Kevin finally could see her genuine care and steady love. He also understood that all his pain from aging and loss of some of the steam he had as a younger man didn't change her appreciation of him.

Through the talk and with a change in medications, his attitude improved, as did his sexual functioning. His job situation didn't improve, but he seemed to adjust to that over time. While still struggling with some depression, Kevin has come to value what he has with Denise and his family. He has also allowed himself to see how much they value him.

Sharing in each other's troubles and problems and working together with a common purpose bonded Denise and Kevin as they have Maureen and me. Today we still work at fulfilling our marital vows: to be patient, kind, and gentle with each other; to cherish and honor one another; to faithfully give ourselves to one another; to sustain each other in both sickness and in health and in times of joy and in times of sadness; to comfort and encourage one another. Sometimes we just need to return to our original vows and life stories and remind ourselves of all that we share, of all that binds us together.

TROUBLE IS A PART OF YOUR LIFE, AND IF YOU DON'T SHARE IT, YOU DON'T GIVE THE PERSON THAT LOVES YOU ENOUGH CHANCE TO LOVE YOU ENOUGH.

Dinah Shore

Share Each Other's Joys and Sorrows

- Plan an evening to view old home movies or videos or to look over old photographs. Share your remembrances of special times you had as a couple and as a family.

- Think back on both positive memories as well as the difficult times. Consider how your lives have blended deeply into one another. Write your reflections of a memory or two. Share them with each other.

- Name a short statement of the philosophy that keeps the two of you together and functioning in tough times.

- In marital vows it is common to hear, "I promise to sustain you in sickness as in health, in poverty as in wealth, in times of joy and in times of sadness—until death." How important is that long-term commitment

as something that provides a depth of sharing for the
two of you?

- The Bible says, "Share each other's troubles and
problems. . . . Don't get tired of doing what is good.
Don't get discouraged and give up, for we will reap
a harvest of blessing at the appropriate time.
Whenever we have the opportunity, we should do
good" (Galatians 6:2, 9-10). How do your own values
and beliefs and those of your partner affect how you
share life together? How do you share in each other's
troubles? each other's joys?

"I" IS SUCH A SLENDER WORD, A
SELFISH WORD. "WE" IS BROADER
AND ENCHANTING FOR IT DOUBLES
THE OUTLOOK.

Mary Paquette

In Sickness and In Health

When Mary was pregnant with their first child, she
and her husband Steve decided that once the
baby was born Mary would stay at home with their
baby. Their first child was a boy. Four other children
followed in rapid succession.

Like most people Mary and Steve had their stresses,
but they carried on facing each challenge the best they
could. Steve had a long commute to and from work and
was away from home for many hours. By the time he
got home from work Mary would usually have already
fed the kids, gotten the boys off to hockey practice, and

the girls off to dance classes. Neither Mary nor Steve particularly liked this situation. But they couldn't see another option, so they dealt with it as best they could. They found themselves sandwiched between the children's needs and the needs of their aging parents, but for the most part they managed fairly well.

Then, over the course of a couple of months, Steve began to experience some unusual physical symptoms. When he finally went to the doctor, a suspicious lump was discovered. After x-rays, the doctor sent him to the hospital. Extensive tests confirmed a tumor that would need surgery. Steve came through surgery successfully, or so the doctors thought. But the surgery left him with bouts of excruciating pain. Two more surgeries were attempted to alleviate his pain, but none proved helpful. Medications were not helping either.

Although Mary and Steve are both thankful that he survived his initial surgery, both admit that Steve's physical pain has brought other challenges to their family. Steve had to quit his job and his disability payments are not nearly enough to pay the bills. Mary has had to carry even more of the parenting load for both of them. The children have learned to help out with chores and other responsibilities. Because noise and commotion can trigger pain for their father they try to keep their sibling squabbling to a minimum.

Only Brent among the children made the situation worse by getting into some serious trouble. First his grades began to slip. Then he started to hang out with new friends of questionable character. Finally, the principal from Brent's school called Mary to say that Brent appeared to be high on narcotics. Mary immediately took him for a blood test which proved those suspicions true.

Mary and Steve were devastated. They enrolled Brent in a chemical dependency treatment program. Mary and Steve started family therapy with all the children. As the kids talked, Steve and Mary realized the extent of their children's anxiety. They also realized how uncomfortable they were in receiving help from friends and family.

"We were taught to be self-sufficient," Mary told one of her friends. "I wish I had asked for help. I think Steve and I have both been denying how bad things were and how tense the kids were."

Lately Brent has been behaving acceptably. The other kids seem fine. The grandparents take the kids places so that Steve and Mary get a break. And now they talk with each other more. Every night as they crawl into bed, they ask each other what they're grateful for from the day. With all the bad news around, they realize that they could get lost in worry and pain. The conversation helps. All their problems weren't solved, but they can admit that in many ways, the problems have drawn them together again—in sickness and in health.

IN EVERYONE'S LIFE, THERE IS A GREAT NEED FOR AN *ANAM CARA*, A SOUL FRIEND. IN THIS LOVE, YOU ARE UNDERSTOOD AS YOU ARE WITHOUT MASK OR PRETENSION. . . . WHERE YOU ARE UNDERSTOOD, YOU ARE AT HOME. UNDERSTANDING NOURISHES BELONGING. WHEN YOU REALLY FEEL UNDERSTOOD, YOU FEEL FREE TO RELEASE YOUR SELF INTO THE TRUST AND SHELTER OF THE OTHER PERSON'S SOUL.

John O'Donohue

In This Together

W hen Bill got home early from work that day he could tell right away who his wife was talking to on the phone. Penny held her head in her hand as her shoulders slumped. Black mascara made two streams down her face as she cried. Bill walked to the phone, took it from her, listened to the raging voice on the other end, and hung it up. Penny got up without speaking and went to wash her face. Over dinner that night neither one brought up the phone call. They had talked about the situation too many times in the past.

After dinner the phone rang again. This time Bill answered. He listened for a short while then he hung it up without speaking to the caller. Penny nervously hung up the dish towel. "Bill, maybe we should go over there. I'd feel just awful if something happened."

Bill watched his wife pace as she dried the dishes. He stood up and put on his coat. "I'm coming with you," she cried as she struggled into her jacket.

They drove silently across town. As they turned onto the dirt road Penny watched Bill's jaw starting to clench. She became more nervous when the little house came into view. No light was on, and the screen door banged open and closed with the wind. They got out and went to the front door. They picked up four newspapers lying against the front step. Inside the door they stepped on piles of mail, and then they smelled the familiar stench. They followed the sound of the heavy breathing. Penny found the light switch. She hesitated. She was not prepared for the sight when she turned on that light. She looked down and winced.

Her mother was passed out on the stained couch, having vomited all over herself. They stepped gingerly through the discarded bottles to pick her up. The stench and matted clothing was almost too much for Penny to bear. As Bill helped Penny get her to the bathroom, he tried to rouse his mother-in-law, "Mable, wake up. Wake up, Mable!"

Mable woke up and immediately hurled a string of obscenities at them. Her arm flung out trying to hit Penny. Bill stood outside the bathroom as Penny tried to wash her mother down. All the while Mable hurled obscenities and terrible accusations at Penny. After Mable was washed and put to bed in clean sheets, Penny and Bill picked up the house. Penny tried to scrub the old couch, but Bill stopped her and dragged the couch to the back door and put it outside.

Penny is the oldest of four siblings, but none of the others have any contact with their abusive mother. Penny's father died of cirrhosis of the liver five years before, and her mother's drinking just got worse. For the last few years they have been trying to get Mable into treatment, but she always refused.

Two weeks after the incident Penny got another one of "those" calls from her mother. Penny knew her mother's drinking habits so well that she could tell right away how many drinks her mother has had and also what type of alcohol she had consumed. Penny could tell it was whiskey because this drink always brought out the tongue lashing. While her mother was in mid-sentence raging over the phone, Penny suddenly heard the phone drop and then an even louder thud. Penny yelled for her mother into the phone but there was no answer.

Penny called 911 on her cell phone as she raced out the door to her mother's home. The paramedics beat Penny to the house. They got Mable to a hospital, but she had suffered a terrible stroke. She survived her stroke, but she would need round-the-clock nursing care. Her drinking days were over.

When Penny and Bill had settled Mable into the nursing home, they walked out feeling relieved.

"Bill, let's go for a walk down by the river. The rosebuds are blooming."

As they strolled among the trees, Penny grabbed Bill's hand. After walking hand in hand for a while, she stopped and looked at her husband. "You know, I can't imagine too many husbands who would clean up their mother-in-law's vomit. You're one heck of a guy, Bill."

"Well, like they say, 'In for a penny, in for a pound,' or is it 'What's good for the goose is good for the gander,' or something like that. Now, let's go get some frozen yogurt. I think that's a fitting way to celebrate the first week of Mable's sobriety!"

EXPERIENCE SHOWS US THAT LOVE DOES NOT CONSIST IN GAZING AT EACH OTHER, BUT IN LOOKING TOGETHER IN THE SAME DIRECTION.

Antoine de Saint-Exupery

MAUREEN ROGERS LAW   LANNY LAW

Marriage and family therapists MAUREEN ROGERS LAW and LANNY LAW are committed to helping people solve the simple and not-so-simple problems that afflict any marriage.

Maureen Rogers Law, who was born and raised in Ireland, received a Master's with a focus on Marriage and Family Therapy from Saint Mary's University of Minnesota. In 1995, she was named Outstanding Graduate Student by the Minnesota Association for Marriage and Family Therapy.

A former minister, Lanny Law received a Master's degree in theological studies from Bethel Seminary in St. Paul, a Master of Divinity degree from McCormick Seminary in Chicago, and a Master's degree with a focus on Conflict Resolution from Saint Mary's University of Minnesota. He also received a Doctor of Ministry Degree in Marriage and Family Counseling from Colgate Rochester Divinity School in Rochester, New York.

The Laws, who have been married for more than 20 years, live with their four children in St. Paul, Minnesota.

Information about Maureen Rogers Law and Lanny Law can be found at **www.TherapistLocator.net**.When reaching this Internet site enter "Lanny Law" and/or "Maureen Law" for their clinic phone number and address, public speaking availability, the types of counseling they each provide, etc. Information about when they are scheduled to make public presentations or appear on radio or television can be found at **www.sorinbooks.com**. When reaching this Internet site enter "Calendar of Events."